A Simple Freedom

The Strong Mind of Robben Island Prisoner No. 468/64

Ahmed Kathrada

with Tim Couzens

Introduction by Nelson Mandela

UNIVERSITY PRESS OF KENTUCKY

"[Friendships] are like those favourite books which always open at the pages we prefer; time has no hold on certain affections; ever new, ever young, they never show signs of age."

Vallery-Radot

Ahmed Kathrada has been so much a part of my life over such a long period. We spent over two decades in jail together, almost all the time on Robben Island. Our stories have become so interwoven, that the telling of one without the voice of the other being heard somewhere would have led to an incomplete narrative.

Kathy's contribution to our liberation struggle and to our movement is well known and well documented. His courage and his commitment to his comrades are legendary. His mature wisdom was an important ingredient of our deliberations and discussions.

What further distinguished him was that he, together with a few other comrades, was an important depository of organisational memory. It is important that the history of our struggle and of our movement be recorded as fully and with all the different perspectives and nuances. Kathy was always analysing and trying to understand, even while he was an active participant.

It is fitting that he now writes this book, giving us all the benefit of his remarkable memory. His words illuminate the ways in which we rose to the challenge facing every prisoner, especially political prisoners, how to survive prison intact, and to emerge from prison undiminished.

PREFACE BY TIM COUZENS

"If you know anything that might be preferable to these maxims, let me hear it; if not, I beg you, make use of these."

Horace, *Epistles*

On a bleak, midwinter morning in 1964, cold, wet, icily windy, seven prisoners were landed by plane on Robben Island, the prison off the coast of Cape Town. They might be described as South Africa's 'magnificent seven' (there was an eighth but he was white and sent elsewhere), though there was nothing magnificent about their physical appearance: they were tired, unshaven and unkempt, and shackled together.

The day before (12 June), in Pretoria, they had been sentenced to life imprisonment at what has come to be known as the Rivonia Trial. They had narrowly escaped the death penalty for their political beliefs and activities against the Nationalist government. Their names were Nelson Mandela, Govan Mbeki, Raymond Mhlaba, Andrew Mlangeni, Elias Motsoaledi and Walter Sisulu. The youngest, at thirty-four, was Ahmed Kathrada.

In the prison register Mandela was famously recorded as prisoner number 466/64. Kathrada was 468/64.

And so began a saga which has become enshrined as a creation story of the modern South Africa. The prisoners were on the island for eighteen years before five of them were moved to Pollsmoor Prison on the mainland until their release in 1989. (Mandela was transferred from Pollsmoor to Victor Verster Prison and released in 1990.)

The story has been told on numerous occasions in various media: this book occupies a modest corner of the overall edifice, a touching and human aspect of one of the main participants.

During his years on the island Ahmed Kathrada ('Kathy' to his friends) jotted down quotations which he came across and liked: proverbs, aphorisms, poetry and drama extracts, and passages from books, magazines and newspapers. This clandestine collection eventually amounted to several thousand items contained in seven exercise books (now housed in the Mayibuye Centre at the University of the Western Cape).

Kathy is not sure himself why he did this. He started the habit as a young school-aged politician when a well-chosen quotation would add authority and gravitas to an impassioned speech in his school's debating society. The Robben Island collection continued the activity precisely because it was forbidden.

The range of selection was circumscribed by the meagreness of the prison library and what few items (such as newspapers) the prisoners could smuggle in or steal from the island rubbish dumps and prison surrounds. Even when they were allowed to pursue graduate studies the prison censors had the last and narrow word on what was allowed.

Nevertheless, the authors represented and the subjects chosen are a rich enough medley. Shaw, Hugo and Dickens, Tolstoy and Twain are favourites, and large chunks of the Greek dramatists are carefully transcribed. Olive Schreiner is honoured; Irish writers (Yeats, O'Casey) are prominent, as is the Indian writer and poet, Tagore, and politicians Gandhi and Nehru.

If, as De Tocqueville suggests in one of the collected quotations, 'the entire man is, so to speak, to be found in the cradle of the child', then Kathy's early years spent within a small enclave of Indian traders and storekeepers surrounded by a dominant world of rural white (mainly Afrikaner) conservatives instilled within him a quiet dignity and an equally quiet hint of wickedness and rebellion. (The majority of the local population was, of course, African.) His relocation at the age of eight to the cauldron of Johannesburg and his introduction to such political mentors as Dr Dadoo, to the Communist Party and to the Passive Resistance Movement produced in him a passionate desire for equality and freedom. He clearly enjoyed – where 'repression sought silence', as James Buchanan phrased it – 'the noise of democracy'.

Many of the quotations concern the arbitrary rule and locked heart of state power (often with poignant appositeness to his own condition): 'When people in power fail to reach a captive's mind, to bend it to their will, they will try to get at it through the body – when they still fail, they mutilate the body' (Vinoba Bhave). Many of them exalt the ability of love and sacrifice to transcend this tyranny.

What did these quotations mean to Kathy? The most obvious answer is that pithy sayings often represent essential and eternal truths, adages to live by and draw comfort from. Comfort, too, from the collective wisdom of many fine minds. There is something more, though.

Proverbs are often the essence or last word of something larger – a folk tale or a parable. Aphorisms often derive from anecdotes. As Cervantes whispered in Kathy's ear on the island, 'a proverb is a short sentence based on long experience'.

Brief reflections are thus made more meaningful by the stories behind them. So, when Kathy wrote down Herodotus's generalised observation that 'great things are achieved through great dangers', he also noted down the larger specific context where the vulnerable Athenians were threatened by the overwhelming power of the Persians.

Consequently, the diary of Anne Frank, circulated surreptitiously on the island, made a huge impression, not just because of what she said but because of the poignancy and courage drawn from the terrible situation in which she found herself, and Kathy preserved several long segments of her diary in his own. In post-prison years he found his own Anne Frank in the life of Michelle Brits, both young girls facing almost inevitable death.

These aphorisms and passages are, sometimes, a shorthand to memory and memory was one of the things that helped Kathy stave off the fear-of-what-might-be during his detention under the new ninety-day detention law prior to the Rivonia Trial. His past came back to him in solitary confinement in what James Joyce might describe as everyday 'epiphanies'. On the Island, these quotations were like familiar friends, gleaned from precious books so difficult to obtain in the restrictive world of the prison.

Friendships, Kathy learned from the writer Vallery-Radot, 'are like those favourite books which always open at the pages we prefer; time has no hold on certain affections; ever new, ever young, they never show signs of age.' For the eighteen years on the island that's all he really had – friendships and books. During the day there was companionship; at night, where silence was the rule, books were, as Robinson Crusoe might say, 'the door of deliverance'.

Each time he opened a book and entered its world a little miracle would have occurred because with the book, as René

Maheu observed, 'the human mind for the first time was able to conquer time and space'. For as long as he was absorbed in a book Kathy could escape into the pelagic expanses of his mind and roam as free as the seagulls outside his cell. The passages he copied, each containing an idea planted in time by his non-corporeal companions, helped steel the soul within the stolen body.

The authorities might control that body but they could not lock up the mind.

These quotations would also remind him that he was not alone in time or space – over two and a half millennia the chorus in Aeschylus's *The Libation Bearers* could still say to Electra that 'thought is free' and across the world in China the Duke of Shao knew, as early as 845 BC, what government's relationship to freedom should be: 'An emperor knows how to govern when poets are free to make verses, people to act plays, historians to tell the truth, ministers to give advice, the poor to grumble at taxes, students to learn lessons aloud, workmen to praise their skill and seek work, people to speak of anything, and old men to find fault with everything.'

If the collection as a whole reveals anything of its compiler through the subjects and examples chosen it is of a man of ideals, interested in love and justice, a man of dignity who, in the teeth of brutality, has retained his natural courtesy. Though, if you are not looking, you might find yourself a prey to his wicked humour.

For a detailed history of his life Kathy's autobiography, *Memoirs*, is a fine read. His *Letters from Robben Island*, neatly composed and beautifully written, is a selection of his prison letters which are immediate and poignant. His part in the tribute to Madiba (the honorary title adopted by elders of Mandela's clan), *Mandela – The Authorised Portrait*, was notable. But there is another way in which he still communicates his experiences – the most personal way of all.

From 1997 until 2006 Kathy served as chairman of the Robben Island Museum Council (the island is now a World Heritage Site) and he has on scores of occasions taken world leaders, celebrities and others on personally conducted visits to the island. It is a great pleasure and extraordinary privilege to be shown round by this courtly man. Not distanced commentary, but living history.

Kathy has never profited from this position or his fame and his satisfaction comes from knowing that thousands of people have gone away from the island with his narrative and his presence imprinted on their memories and that, more than anyone, he has spread the living story through the world and ensured the future memory of the island. This unobtrusive service has not always had the recognition it deserves for the contribution it has made to collective memory.

For those who never have the opportunity to tour in person with Kathy, this book, fusing visual images, a selection of his collected quotations, and momentary epiphanies of his own memories, collected in informal conversations, offers readers a chance to accompany him, in a personal and friendly way, on a journey to the island.

"Prometheus, for his services, was invited to dine with the Olympian gods. There, in pity for the sad plight of mankind, he stole a spark of divine fire and conveyed it to the earth. He taught man all the uses of fire, and in particular how to melt metal and shape it into weapons and tools. Zeus, angered that divine supremacy should be so imperilled, demanded repentance and complete submission from Prometheus. When the champion of mankind proved defiant, Zeus sent Hephaestus, the Olympian fire god, to chain him to a rocky peak in the

Caucasus mountains. (See *Prometheus Bound*.) Prometheus continued his defiance of tyranny and reinforced it by declaring that he knew an ancient prophecy, revealed to him by his mother, the earth (the original holder of all foreknowledge) which threatened the ultimate downfall of Zeus unless he should be warned in time. For a thousand years Prometheus endured the successive torments which Zeus inflicted to make him reveal the prophecy; until at last Zeus turned from violence to reason and offered Prometheus release and pardon."

Notes from the introduction to *Aeschylus: The Oresteian Trilogy* by Philip Vellacott

I survived three circles of hell – the ninety-day detention, a trial for treason and sabotage, and years and years of imprisonment. Each demanded its own accommodation: the first required inner strength for naked survival; the second, principle over legality and expediency; the last, discipline and endurance.

The ninety-day detention law, sanctioned by the General Law Amendment Act of 1963, was one of the cruellest of the apartheid laws. It allowed solitary confinement for all but one hour per day for ninety days (later one hundred and eighty, then indefinitely) giving the security police almost unlimited power. Many detainees were tortured or killed, or simply disappeared.

I am arrested along with ANC (African National Congress) leaders Walter Sisulu, Govan Mbeki and Raymond Mhlaba almost immediately after the Act's promulgation. (Mandela is already on Robben Island, serving a five-year sentence.) We are strictly forbidden from talking to one another. When the metal grille slams shut I am alone, like I've never been in all my life.

The cell is small, there are two thin soiled mats on the floor to sleep on, a bucket for ablutions, a metal plate and spoon, a window too high to see out of and a single naked light bulb, like a demented Cyclops, staring impassively and relentlessly at me day and night. In the evening I am given a plastic bottle of water. This is life stripped to its barest.

In the morning we are allowed to shower and exercise in the so-called 'church hall' with our comrades, walking around in single file, bound to silence. There are no women ... no children ... no gardens ... it is nature strangled; a monastic life which has not been chosen.

After a few days, pacing my cell like a worn tiger in a squalid cage, I long for someone to talk to. The only company I get (erratically over the weeks) are my interrogators, one friendly and affable, the other, the dreaded Swanepoel, small-eyed, mean, brutal, calculating, but with his anger and hatred always threatening to boil over.

They want information. They offer salvation. At a price.

I am told in no uncertain terms, 'We've got you at last, and now you've nowhere else to go. You are going to hang!'

❋

I am Ahmed Kathrada. The Kathradas come from north-western India and are Gujerati-speaking, as was my mother's family. But I am a second-generation South African, born and bred in a country which has an extraordinary and turbulent history. I have looked into some of the darker corners of its soul. I have seen the dark side of the land and I have seen the brighter side.

I spent twenty-six continuous years of my life in prison (one in detention in Pretoria, eighteen on Robben Island, seven in Pollsmoor). Afterwards, in the first fully democratic election in South Africa, I was elected as a Member of Parliament and was appointed Parliamentary Counsellor in the office of President Mandela.

I live both in Johannesburg (where I am on the board of the Nelson Mandela Foundation) and, rather more, in Cape Town with my partner Barbara, herself an MP who spent nine years as a political prisoner.

I am often courted by the media and frequently accompany individuals or parties of people to the island. I am free to make these choices and say what I like where once I was not.

When I started out in life it was a very different world and it should never be forgotten how hard these freedoms were come by (and how they should be cherished).

❋

I was born in 1929 in Schweizer-Reneke, a small agricultural town two hundred and forty kilometres south-west of Johannesburg, South Africa's equivalent of the Deep South in the United States. It was dry and dusty, on the edge of the Kalahari Desert, and always threatened by drought, which seemed to match the puritan conservatism of the mainly Afrikaner farmers who dominated the community. The local Africans eked out a meagre living, a few as sharecroppers but most as farm labourers.

My father was a shopkeeper, comfortable but not wealthy. The Indian community was small and, given the political and social circumstances, forced to be somewhat insular, and had to tread carefully, though my father was held in respect by many. The Afrikaner community was deeply racist but not entirely monolithic. In the house to the left of us lived the bank manager, behind us was a former mayor. The midwife who delivered me, Ouma Oosthuizen, lived not far away. Though never forswearing her strong allegiance to the Nationalist Party, which entrenched apartheid when it came to power, Ouma was not only a customer in the shop but a frequent visitor and family friend who was like a 'granny' or godmother to me. She must have instilled in me early on that individuals often surprise and contradict stereotype.

Compelled to be insular (Indians could not own land), my early family life was a sheltered and happy one giving me a strong sense of emotional security. My parents were very religious and their Muslim faith, though no one would say it in so many words, made us feel we were somewhat special and gave us an inner strength.

As a child, of course, politics was not in the forefront of my days but I vividly remember the curfew bell that rang at nine o'clock every night, signalling the time after which Africans needed a pass to be on the streets.

But at the age of eight the laws of segregation changed my life forever. In Schweizer-Reneke there were separate schools for whites and separate schools for Africans and (being Indian) I could go to none of them.

I was sent to Johannesburg to live with my aunt. So politics dispatched me to the city and that is where I learned *my* politics at a very early age. While still a schoolboy I was distributing leaflets and chalking freedom slogans on walls.

Prison is a state of mind. If you go into prison with a negative state of mind and spend your days with that same negative state of mind it's going to be hell. Fortunately, my early adult years were a kind of apprenticeship for solitary incarceration.

As a young activist in the Passive Resistance Movement of 1946 I served a month's imprisonment at the age of seventeen, and in the 1952 Defiance Campaign I was among the twenty activists and leaders who were convicted and received a nine-month suspended sentence.

In 1954 I had been banned from gatherings and from membership of a number of organisations. Then in 1956 I was arrested along with one hundred and fifty-five other activists and Congress leaders. Thirty of us, of the original 156, were eventually tried for treason in what would become known as the Treason Trial. The notorious trial lasted until 1961 when we were all finally acquitted. In 1962 I was the second person placed under house arrest, after anti-apartheid leader Helen Joseph.

House arrest turned my flat into a prison. I had to be indoors from 6 p.m. to 7 a.m. next morning and from 6 p.m. Friday until 7 a.m. Monday. No visitors were allowed. I'm not antisocial, I'm gregarious, so the first months were very difficult. Even my mother was not allowed to visit me at the flat. I met her once, in November 1962, when I went down (illegally) to the car to see her. That was my very last meeting with her.

Then, the following year, my political superiors took a decision that was to change both my immediate future and my entire life. I was instructed to go underground and live the life of an outlaw. (I refused the option of exile outside the country.)

For several months I avoided capture, living at times disguised as a Portuguese under an alias. On 11 July 1963, along with other senior members of the Congress Movement (an amalgam of African, Indian, coloured and white anti-apartheid organisations) I was at Liliesleaf Farm in Rivonia north of Johannesburg to discuss a controversial document of the resistance movement (Operation Mayibuye). We were caught in a surprise raid by the South African Special Branch, accompanied by armed uniformed police and dogs.

Instinct told me I must make a run for it – against all the odds. Instinctive, but amateurish. Walter Sisulu and I were ordered to stop in our tracks. Which we did.

We were all taken first to the Old Fort jail in Johannesburg and then transferred to Pretoria Local Prison to start a period of ninety days of solitary confinement. Here came the first real test – to establish one's state of mind and assert one's dignity.

❄

It is July and knife-cold. There's an open courtyard and showers. Incoming prisoners are forced to shower before registration. I have had cold showers before in summer but never in winter. The senior police and prison officers are arranged around the courtyard watching, gleeful, mocking. The master race at play.

This is the blunt end of the weapon the state brandishes to deprive people of their self-respect.

When my turn comes I run in and run straight out. They don't give us towels, we have to use handkerchiefs. My relationship with the police has always been bad so one of the security policemen complains to the colonel in charge and I am ordered back in.

This is a moment of utter humiliation. It is also a critical moment, one of the most important of my life. I can succumb to the indignity or I can resist. At stake is my psychological freedom, the freedom of my mind. I am Ahmed Kathrada. That is who I am. I walk slowly back into the shower and stand there under a cold, indifferent sky for as long as it takes to remove the smirk from their faces and for me to steel my independence.

The habit of taking a daily cold shower has remained with me to this day, a continuity of that pride.

All human beings experience fear at some stage in their lives. There are childhood fears, and adult fears. For children it is mostly induced fear: 'If you are naughty, such and such will happen.' Fear of spooks; fear of fire; fear of some animals, insects and reptiles. These are mostly ephemeral; they either diminish with time, or they disappear.

Adult fear is different. It is not imaginary; it is self-experienced, or learnt from the experiences of others. It is ever present. In the apartheid years African people lived in constant fear of being raided and arrested by the police at any time of the day or night, either under the repressive pass laws, or for possessing illegal liquor. Hundreds of thousands of African people were jailed for transgressions of these laws.

I'm in complete solitary confinement for ninety days, as complete as my captors can make it. No visits to look forward to, because no visitors, not even lawyers, are allowed. No books or newspapers to help me while away time, because all reading matter is prohibited. No letters to and from my people, because no letters are permitted. Apart from routine interruption by the sounds of the locking and unlocking of cell doors by warders, and the ominous visits by security police interrogators, I have only my thoughts for company.

There is one terrible night in solitary confinement. The wing where the four of us are kept in separate cells is shut off from the rest of the prison. The section door crashes open and a new prisoner is admitted – Zeph Mothopeng, an elderly and respected leader of the Pan African Congress (PAC). He is clearly in great distress, tortured to within an inch of his life, broken in body and mind, and suffering a mental breakdown. Incoherent, he shouts, makes speeches, sings, cries, bangs on the door and kicks the wall. All night long his screams fill our cells and pierce our hearts. Next morning I see the fresh lesions on his fingers from the electric shocks.

❋

One clear morning at exercise one of our comrades whispers that Looksmart Ngudle, an ANC activist from Cape Town and only the second ninety-day detainee, has been tortured to death under interrogation.

Is this to be my fate? Will I break under torture? In the dark night of the body is there any room for the soul?

Locked in my cell, my only companions and my only resource for days and weeks are my thoughts.

But soon, and to my amazement, something happens. In my isolation there is an explosion of memory. One after the other, things just start to come to me. My childhood returns – my late father, my mother, my only sister, my four brothers, my nieces, nephews and their spouses, my friends, my comrades. My father died when I was fourteen so I had never really come to know him fully, or my mother. But some of the lessons I learnt from him remain indelible in my mind, and stand me in good stead. The most important being to treat all people, regardless of colour, with respect. He reminds me. I am Ahmed Kathrada. That is who I am.

Memory is what sustains: joy, happiness, comfort, loved ones. Long-forgotten incidents, songs, poems, nursery rhymes, prose – all these come back to me. What wonderful company. I pace up and down my tiny cell, singing, reciting.

I even remember all the jokes of my youth and the practical jokes my brother used to play. But most inspiring, and directly relevant to my situation, the most important of all, I recall the struggle songs that I learned in the Young Communist League – songs of courage, of martyrdom, of victory. I want to drink in, and live the words of Irish hero, Kevin Barry, when he challenges his executioners: 'Shoot me like an Irish soldier; do not hang me like a dog; for I fought for Ireland's freedom, on that bright September morn ...'

I think a lot about the struggle of the All India Congress against British rule in that country. While I cannot recall the exact words of Congress leader Subhas Chandra Bose, I can readily identify with the gist of them, because he decided to organise a 'Liberation Army' to fight the British: 'If you wish to enjoy the beauty of the dawn, you must be prepared to live through the dark hours of the night ... If you wish to smell the aroma of the full-blown rose, you must accept the thorns ... If you wish to enjoy the fruits of freedom, you have to endure struggle and sacrifice ...'

I feel the warmth of the powerful prose of India's greatest poet, Rabindranath Tagore, particularly 'The Bankruptcy of European Civilisation'; stir to the inspiration of Lincoln's Gettysburg Address; and wrap myself in the unforgettable, and most immediately relevant, words of Jawaharlal Nehru: '... fear builds its phantoms which are more fearsome than reality itself, and reality when calmly analysed, and its consequences willingly accepted, loses much of its terror ...'

I derive comfort, strength and courage from the fact that thoughts do not need passports. No warder or security policeman is going to stop me – even from thinking aloud!

Best of all, I'm alive in this little world I've created in my thoughts. I'm learning to tackle fear. I'm deciding to fight it. I drum up enough courage to confront, when he comes, the brute – police-interrogator Swanepoel – in his own language. I remind him of the words of the Afrikaans poet, Cilliers, who powerfully pronounced his admiration for the man who has the courage to stand up for himself *('Ek hou van 'n man wat sy man kan staan')* and to stand by his fellow men. And I ask Swanepoel, when he hears words like these, how can he find it in himself to ask me to betray my comrades?

❊

There are one or two lighter moments. I am allowed to have the Bible – and read it several times, learning much about Christianity and its history – but not the Koran. (Some time later, on Robben Island, I ask a warder for a Koran, and he says '*Koerant?* How can you ask for a *koerant* when you know it is not allowed?' A *koerant* is a newspaper in Afrikaans and I don't know if he is being funny, or just ignorant.)

There is an occasion when something happens to Govan Mbeki which propels my nights and days to new heights of fear. I notice his black hair turning white, and my immediate suspicion is that he has been tortured. I have more sleepless nights, coupled with fresh fears. Has he broken down? Has he spoken? And, more importantly, has he spoken about me? But I'm unable to communicate with him. I'm completely frustrated. But as happens now and then, there are brief moments – in the exercise hall and the bathroom – when we manage to exchange a few words, and I ask him, 'Why is your hair turning white?' He says, 'Nothing to worry about. My black hair dye has worn off, and I can't replenish my supply!'

❋

Memory reminds us of who we are, gives us a sense of self and its steadfastness, and helps us to be free.

My strength and hope help me survive the ninety gruelling, gruesome days. Then, almost as suddenly as it began, on 7 October 1963, comes the end of my solitary detention.

We are going to see our lawyers; but we don't know who they are. Neither do they know who their clients are going to be. We are taken to the consulting room. But before that, they bring in Mandela. He's wearing short pants and sandals. He has completed eleven months of his five-year sentence, and he's lost weight. But his bearing and his presence are unshakeable. Rusty Bernstein, Denis Goldberg, James Kantor and Bob Hepple have been brought from the white section of the prison. We now know who our fellow accused are going to be.

One of the lawyers, Joel Joffe, years later, recalled this consultation: 'We had come on legal business to consult the accused. But it was clear that they were in no mood for consultation. They were rediscovering, it seemed to us, the joys of speech, not unlike people who had been dumb and had suddenly had the power of speech restored to them ... they were drunk with speech, with human communication and contact, and being able to talk, to meet with and touch other people, too involved in all these new sensations, too intoxicated with them to be prepared to consider serious problems of law ...'

A day or so afterwards we have our first serious consultation. Each of us, in his own way, has given thought as to how the case should be conducted. We have to bear in mind that among the accused we have four of the most senior leaders of the African National Congress and Umkhonto we Sizwe (the military wing of the movement, known as MK) – Madiba, Walter, Govan, Raymond. On their shoulders lies the gravest responsibility. The eyes of the world are on the upcoming trial. The members of the ANC, and the oppressed people in the country, are looking up to them. If they succumb, and plead for mercy, it would be the most severe blow to the liberation movement, and would set us back decades. We have to conduct ourselves in a way that will boost the people's morale, and instil in them a sense of pride in the ANC. They must be able to walk tall.

Therefore, there is little debate when Madiba suggests that this is not a legal but a political trial, and that it has to be fought politically. Our advantage is that our defence team fully agree with our approach. This is after cautioning us to prepare for the worst. They don't spell it out, but the meaning is clear – the gallows.

Although there is, in my case, little evidence against me, I have a special responsibility. I am an Indian, belonging to one of the minority groups. The South African Indian Congress leaders, Dr Dadoo and Dr Naicker, had signed a pact of unity with the ANC's president, Dr Xuma, in 1947. This was not just a pact on paper, but had already been implemented in the Defiance Campaign of 1952 and in the Congress of the People conference of 1955 where South Africa's Freedom Charter was adopted. Indians were co-accused in the Defiance Campaign Trial of 1952 and the marathon Treason Trial of 1956–61. Indian Congress members were among the first to join MK and were among the first to be arrested and sent to Robben Island. And now, it is no accident that I'm with Madiba, Walter and others in the Rivonia Trial. Come what may, I dare not show weakness;

I must face the court with pride, and not in any way be apologetic. I must reiterate our political beliefs. Under no circumstances should I do or say anything that sets me apart from my colleagues. When Madiba suggests that when we are found guilty, and even sentenced to death, we should not appeal, I wholeheartedly agree, knowing what that means.

So Madiba speaks for me, too, when at the trial, he makes one of history's most dramatic speeches: 'During my lifetime I have dedicated myself to this struggle of the African people. I have fought against white domination and I have fought against black domination. I have cherished the ideal of a democratic and free society in which all persons live together in harmony and with equal opportunities. It is an ideal which I hope to live for and to achieve ...

"But, if needs be, it is an ideal for which I am prepared to die."

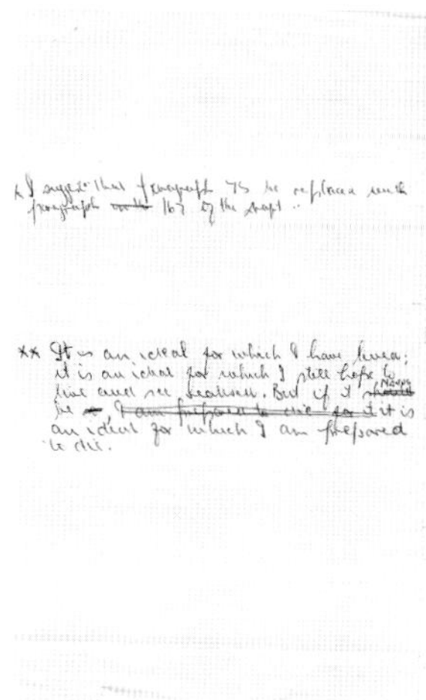
* I suggest that paragraph 75 be replaced with paragraph 167 of the draft.

** It is an ideal for which I have lived; it is an ideal for which I still hope to live and see realised. But if needs be it is an ideal for which I am prepared to die.

The great nineteenth-century prison reformer Elizabeth Fry has wise advice for all societies: 'When thee builds a prison, thee had better build with the thought ever in thy mind that thee and thy children may occupy the cells.'

The Nationalist government which came to power in 1948 certainly did not give this much thought. If it is true that a prison is a mirror of the society that makes it, then the brutality of ninety days' detention together with the inhuman treatment of prisoners on Robben Island and elsewhere offered little comfort for those outside.

Apartheid South Africa, with an avalanche of institutionalised race laws, many borrowed from Hitler's Third Reich –

Race Classification, Separate Amenities, Bantu Education, Mixed Marriages, Group Areas – turned the whole country into an open prison for millions. I was forcibly reminded of this in the few days before the verdict of our trial was announced. A warder asked me, is all your suffering necessary when you could lead a comfortable life outside? How could I explain my feelings to him? What good are these comforts when I haven't got dignity? What is life without dignity? That very morning I had learnt that, because of the Group Areas Act, the house where I was born and where my father settled had to be abandoned. Not because of any road or town development project, nor for hygienic reasons or slum clearances, but simply because we were Indians and our house happened to be next to the Dutch Reformed Church (even though the house was built before the church).

On my first visit to my birthplace after my release in 1989, I paused before the vacant lot where that happy childhood home had been. It had been razed to the ground.

My mother died while I was in prison. This had been her home for which my parents had worked so hard and sacrificed so much. My brother Ismail, who also lived there, died not long after the family was forced to move.

The day I got the news about my brother I sat a long time in my cell thinking of his last visit to me on the island and I wrote to his daughter, my niece, Zohrabibi: 'Already at that time he must have had some premonition of his approaching death. I feel certain that what hastened his death was being forced to move from the house to which he was so attached ... After having literally grown up in that house, it became part of himself ... He must have been living there with millions of happy memories ... And then finally when he was wrenched away from that house by cruel, unfeeling people, he was suddenly a lost man. Little did they care that they were destroying not just bricks and mortar, but they had passed a slow death sentence on a healthy, live, guiltless human being.'

As I looked at the weeds where the house had once stood, myself at last a free man, with my own memories, I felt as though a large part of me had been unfairly taken away and the pain was great. I wanted somehow to retrieve the past, and those who peopled it, and bring it back, whole and healed.

In the early years of our imprisonment the government did everything it could to break our spirit. We were treated brutally (though not physically assaulted as were our comrades in the communal cells). Later, conditions improved somewhat though they were never acceptable. What got us through was our inner resolve, our discipline, and a determination, in the teeth of perverse opposition, to study and increase our knowledge and understanding.

In prison one needs to assert little freedoms to preserve the vision of a 'greater freedom'. When I was finally released on 15 October 1989, I took with me many cardboard cartons. The prized possessions were my *Oxford Book of English Verse* and Shakespeare's *Complete Works,* which I had managed to keep with me through six prisons, as well as nine hundred carbon copies of letters I had written and an equivalent number received. There were also the seven notebooks of quotations. One of the reasons I had kept them was that whenever I jotted a quotation down it simply made me feel better.

During my imprisonment, I had been deprived of my study privileges on several occasions as punishment for some transgression or other. Every book, except the Bible, and every bit of paper, including the illicit notebooks, was taken away. This was particularly severe when the Mandela manuscript (which was the basis of what became his famous autobiography, *Long Walk to Freedom*) was uncovered in the garden. My material and that of my colleagues was locked in an empty cell at the head of the corridor.

One Sunday, the warders who were normally in charge had the weekend off. The replacement warders were not familiar with our routine and did not know about the storage cell. My friend Laloo Chiba and I persuaded one of them to unlock it so we could, we said, clean it. We did clean it – out – of everything I needed. It was not stealing, it was repossession, an act of liberation. And the regular warders were none the wiser when they returned to work on Monday.

So the quotation notebooks, physically, in themselves, are literal representatives of freedom as well as containing in their writings the free thoughts of the greatest minds.

During our 1963 trial I wrote in a letter (smuggled out and therefore uncensored) to Sylvia, the brave and committed woman I was then in love with, that I felt that change was inevitable and there were bound to be cracks in the granite of the apartheid state. How long the wait would be was difficult to predict. I felt that change was imminent. I was right about the cracks but wrong about the imminence. The long wait for liberty taught me much.

Freedom – vulnerable, in need of eternal vigilance and priceless above rubies – is like a beautiful woman, standing unconscious of her beauty and serene in an angry sea, the still centre of the churning world. But if you look closely she, too, in infinitely complex, infinitely slow and subtle ways, is changing, like an island with a history.

JUTA
1853
Stenographer's
Note Book
Specially manufactured for —
JUTA & Co. LTD.
Court Road,
Wynberg,
Phone 779191
Church Street,
Cape Town,
Phone 24548
Ref. A109.
Wiro Binding
Always keeps flat — open or closed

"When thee builds a prison, thee had better build with the thought ever in mind that thee and thy children may occupy the cells."

Elizabeth Fry

> "Sceptreless, free, uncircumscribed, but man
> Equal, unclassed, tribeless and nationless,
> Exempt from awe, worship, degree, the king
> Over himself; just, gentle, wise, but man."

Shelley, *Prometheus Unbound*

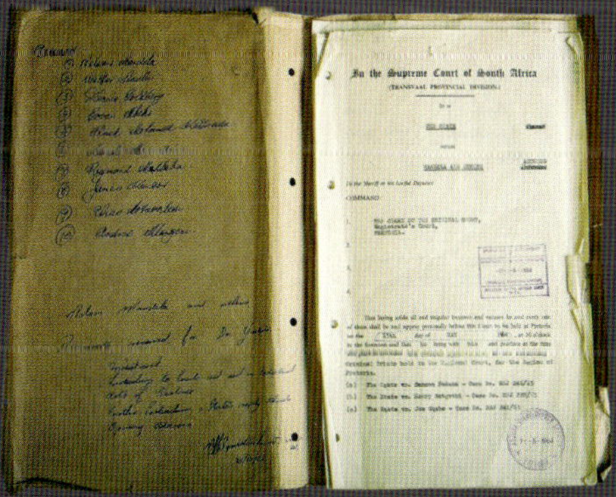

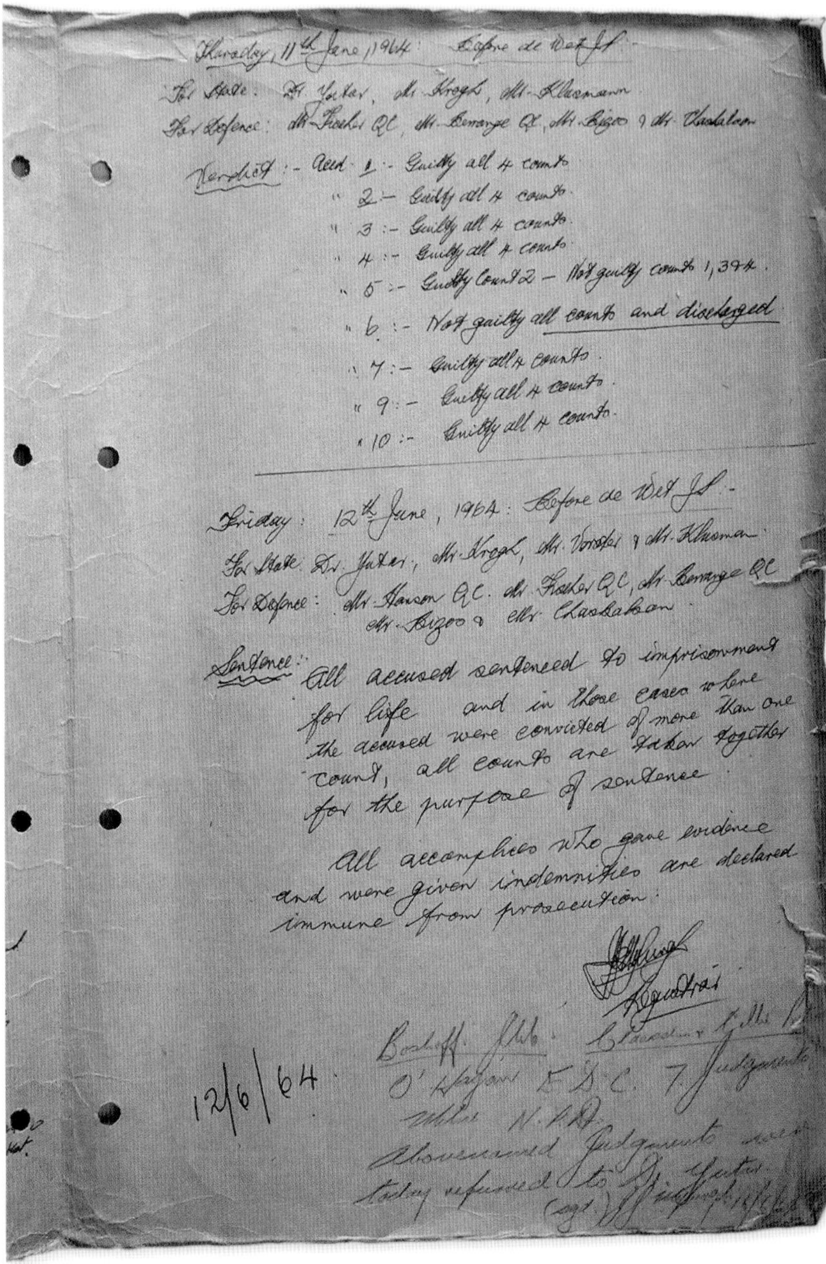
Thursday, 11th June 1964: Before de Wet JP

For State: Dr Yutar, Mr Krogh, Mr Kleinmann

For Defence: Mr Fischer QC, Mr Berrange QC, Mr Bizos & Mr Chaskalson

Verdict:- Accd. 1:- Guilty all 4 counts

" 2:- Guilty all 4 counts.

" 3:- Guilty all 4 counts.

" 4:- Guilty all 4 counts

" 5:- Guilty Count 2 — Not guilty counts 1, 3 & 4.

" 6:- Not guilty all counts and discharged

" 7:- Guilty all 4 counts.

" 9:- Guilty all 4 counts.

" 10:- Guilty all 4 counts.

Friday: 12th June, 1964: Before de Wet JP.

For State: Dr Yutar, Mr Krogh, Mr Vorster & Mr Kleinman

For Defence: Mr Hanson QC. Mr Fischer QC, Mr Berrange QC, Mr Bizos & Mr Chaskalson

Sentence: All accused sentenced to imprisonment for life and in those cases where the accused were convicted of more than one count, all counts are taken together for the purpose of sentence.

All accomplices who gave evidence and were given indemnities are declared immune from prosecution.

[illegible] Registrar

12/6/64 [illegible] 7 Judgments [illegible] Abovenamed Judgments were today refused to Dr Yutar. (sgd.) [illegible]

[The back page of the Rivonia Trial charge sheet listing the verdict against each of the accused.]

01.

"There has been, there is, no silence like the silence in a court

when the judge lifts his head to hand down judgement. All other communication, within and without, is stilled; all is ended. This is the last word."

Nadine Gordimer, *The House Gun*

[01.

We were found guilty on 11 June. Sentence would be passed the next day.

I don't know how much I slept that night. I can't recall any more, but one thing I can say is that we knew no apartheid court was going to change the death sentence if it were imposed. Even though there was less evidence against me, I was found guilty of being in the conspiracy. Death was going to mean death.

That morning we were taken to court. What I remember was, there was this criminal who had been facing the death sentence. He was guilty of a whole series of rape and murder charges. I don't think we could have travelled with him; we may have just met him there. And he was praying for us! 'You know I pray for you people every day,' he assured us.

In court there was a general expectation of the death sentence for all of us. Your mind goes back to that. Complete silence.

Judge de Wet was very nervous. He just passed sentence and virtually ran out.

His voice was very soft, hanging faintly in the air. The spectators didn't hear what the sentence was, so Denis Goldberg shouted across to them, 'Life'.

That was quite a moment.]

"One takes half a lifetime

to perceive some of the obvious facts about liberty: that total liberty does not exist and, even if it did, nobody would want it; that it only has reality in terms of the qualifications, 'from what?', 'to do what?'; and that most people knock their brains out in pursuit of human relationships which will in one sense restrict their liberty, but in another and more important sense expand it by freeing them from themselves. It takes but a short time in jail to discover the value of liberty in its most primitive form. It is so precious that even a grain of it makes the blood pound and the heart sing."

Cedric Belfrage, British author and journalist deported from the US during the McCarthy era – among other things he reported on the execution for espionage of Ethel and Julius Rosenberg in 1953

[02.

Arbitrary and unpredictable behaviour is part of tyranny's cruel game.

What they did to us – this was Friday – was say, 'You'll see your visitors tomorrow and your lawyers on Tuesday in Pretoria.'

So we went to bed and the prison authorities said, 'Tonight we're going to put you all together; you've got a lot of food and we'll give you a chance to eat it because tomorrow you'll eat prison food.' So they kept us in the same cell for the first time since our arrest.

That very night, past midnight, it was bitterly cold, they suddenly came, unlocked the door and said, 'Dress up.' We asked, 'What's happening?' They said, 'We don't know. Just dress up.'

Handcuffed – I was chained to Govan Mbeki with leg irons. They put us in a plane at a military airport. We were escorted by the prison authorities and the police; some military people were there as well.

On Saturday morning we landed on Robben Island, the seven of us.]

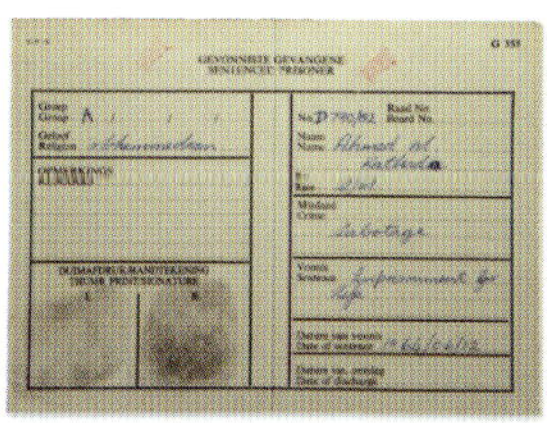
GEVONNISTE GEVANGENE
SENTENCED PRISONER

Group A

Religion

Name

Crime

Sentence

Date of sentence

Date of discharge

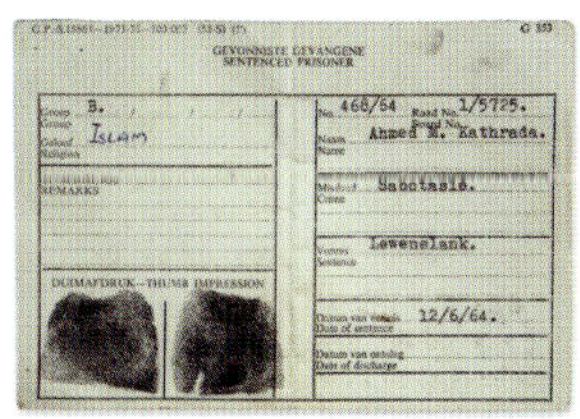
G 353

GEVONNISTE GEVANGENE
SENTENCED PRISONER

Group B.

Religion Islam

REMARKS

No. 468/64 Board No. 1/5725.

Name Ahmed M. Kathrada.

Crime Sabotasie.

Sentence Lewenslank.

Datum van vonnis / Date of sentence 12/6/64.

Datum van ontslag / Date of discharge

DUIMAFDRUK—THUMB IMPRESSION

[03.

EsiQithini ('The Island'), to which we were consigned, has a long history of pain. In the seventeenth and eighteenth centuries it was a place of imprisonment, slavery, banishment and exile. In the nineteenth, several great African chiefs were imprisoned there, and it has variously hosted a lunatic asylum and a leper colony, all accompanied by unspeakable suffering.

After serving as a military base during the Second World War it came under the aegis of the Department of Prisons and the maximum-security prison was finished in 1964.

When Garrison penned his outrage there were historical similarities between the conditions of black people in America and South Africa. Both countries had a grim history of slavery. In 1833 slavery was abolished in the Cape but racial discrimination did not vanish with it.

It is disturbing to think too, that, even in the twenty-first century, slavery exists throughout the world, even if in some cases in the disguised form of the human trafficking of children and women. It is a scourge that Garrison would have faced with equal revulsion.]

03.

"I will be as harsh as truth, and as uncompromising as justice.

On this subject I do not wish to think, or speak, or write with moderation. No! No! Tell a man whose house is on fire to give a moderate alarm; tell him to moderately rescue his wife from the hands of a ravisher; tell the mother to gradually extricate her babe from the fire into which it has fallen – but urge me not to use moderation in a cause like the present. I am in earnest – I will not equivocate – I will not excuse – I will not retreat a single inch – and I will be heard."

William Lloyd Garrison, principal leader of the 'Abolitionists' (of slavery) in North America, 1831

Quota

"In prison one needs to assert little freedoms to preserve the vision of a 'greater freedom'. When I was finally released on 15 October 1989, I took with me many cardboard cartons. The prized possessions were my *Oxford Book of English Verse* and Shakespeare's *Complete Works,* which I had managed to keep with me through six prisons, as well as nine hundred carbon copies of letters I had written and an equivalent number received. There were also the seven notebooks of quotations. One of the reasons I had kept them was that whenever I jotted a quotation down it simply made me feel better."

04.

"If I had to use a single word to define life on Robben Island, it would be 'cold'. Cold food, cold showers, cold winters, cold wind coming in off the sea, cold warders, cold cells, cold comfort … It was as if the cold had somehow permeated our very bones, and we never quite managed to thaw out again."

Ahmed Kathrada, *Memoirs*

[04.

I quickly learnt that, unlike the rest of South Africa, Cape Town has a Mediterranean climate. This means that not only do we have rain in winter, but that it is accompanied by cold and a fierce wind. And stormy seas. Altogether miserable.

On our arrival we were housed in the old prison because the construction of the newly built single-cell 'B' section was not quite complete. But as far as our jailors were concerned, this was of little importance, and we were soon moved into 'B' section, with the wall-paint not completely dry, and the smell of wet cement still clinging to some cells. Guided by a desire to make life as unbearable as possible, an instruction had gone out to the builders to remove the two top window panes, so that more cold air could freely penetrate our cells. There were no beds (not for fourteen years); we slept on the floor on two mats with three thin blankets. Most prisoners slept in their clothes, some even in their boots.

The most callous and cruel part of the apartheid mentality not only violated basic human rights, but also sanctified the belief, which it sought to justify on biblical grounds, that God had endowed on the white race a position in life that was superior to all people who were not white. In practice this meant that Mandela, because he was African, would not get bread, and his ration of sugar, meat and fish would be less than mine (being Indian), while mine was less than that of Denis Goldberg in his separate white prison in Pretoria. And Mandela had to wear short trousers, through the hottest summer and the coldest winter, while I was given long pants. This fits in with Orwell's observation that some people are more equal than others. If there was anything designed to engender hatred, it was to see our elders and leaders – Walter Sisulu, Govan Mbeki – twenty years my senior, shivering and suffering from the cold. And we had to look on helplessly. J

"Not unto us, but unto the noble army of the heroic dead

be the praise, the glory, and the laurels of the divine liberty that purifies the earth, the sea and the air. Greater love knoweth no man than the love of the soldier who lays down his life for the unborn generations of mankind."

James Douglas

[05.

Memory is fundamental. It is on the memory of the past that the present is built and it will be on the memory of the present that the future will be built.

You can take all the deprivation, all the suffering, but the greatest sacrifice, in our case, was the comrades who were hanged or tortured to death, and when we got news of these deaths it was terrible.

Babla Saloojee was like a brother to me. We were very close. He was gentle; he was courageous – some people would say he was reckless.

We used to go around at night putting up posters. It wasn't dangerous but it was illegal. One night we had finished and had one poster left, so he said, 'Let's put it up at Gray's Building.' I said, 'No man, that's ...' So he said, 'I'll put it up,' and he did. Gray's Building was the headquarters of the security police in Johannesburg. Years later, on the island, Walter had his first visit from his wife, Albertina. She was sombre. Babla was dead.

He had been interrogated and tortured by the brutal 'Rooi Rus' Swanepoel. Before he died he smuggled out a message to his wife, 'Pray for me.' He was thrown from the seventh floor of Gray's Building, where he had, years before, mischievously posted our last poster.

After the mass killing of African protesters by police at Sharpeville in 1960, Babla was the first in a long list of martyrs – among them Ruth First, Steve Biko, Jeanette Schoon and her young daughter, along with many, many others.

There are some pieces of news one would prefer not to get in prison.]

"In the Nazi concentration camp,

the basic message of fairy stories stayed with me: that in life you encounter terrible events, but if you can hold on to your values, you might survive and be the better for it."

Professor Bruno Bettelheim

[06.

In prison, as in concentration camps and similar places of punishment and deprivation, the human and material values of inmates are constantly put to the test. One is constantly exposed to temptations that could make life less intolerable.

In our jails, and on Robben Island, the circumstances and choices were not as ghastly and grim as the Nazi concentration camps (except when one was in the hands of the security police) but our prisons were no beds of roses and rank-and-file inmates, as well as leaders, were exposed to temptations of one sort or another.

On Robben Island, Madiba was a great inspiration.

Soon after our arrival, Madiba was called to the office and offered preferential treatment: he would have an improved diet, as well as exemption from work and the right to wear long trousers. He refused. When it came to hunger strikes the ANC had decided to exempt our senior people who were old, and possibly not in good health. Again he, Madiba, Walter and others refused. They took part in the hunger strikes, and came to work with us at the quarry, working with pick and shovels.

In 1977, in the hope of gaining credibility for the so-called independent Transkei Bantustan (one of the government-designated African 'homelands'), Madiba was offered release from prison provided he settled in the Transkei. He refused, maintaining that the whole of South Africa was his homeland.

In 1982, before my transfer to Pollsmoor Prison, out of the blue I was singled out for a special offer. The government was prepared to release me if I agreed to certain conditions. I refused.

Again, in 1985, President Botha offered to release all political prisoners who were prepared to renounce violence. Five of us were at Pollsmoor at the time. Again, under Madiba's leadership, we rejected the offer of a conditional release.

This type of exemplary behaviour was a tremendous morale-booster for all of us. The leaders led from the front, and suffered whatever consequences followed.]

"I believe only in the purifying fire of self sacrifice

can the dross of selfishness be consumed and the greatness of the human soul set free."

From Charles Chaplin's *My Autobiography*

"Without the power to sacrifice

self, great ideas will never bear fruit."

Louis Michel at the burial of Blanqui, 1881

[07.

We worked with hammers for the first six months, sitting on blocks of concrete, breaking big stones into smaller stones, and the smaller stones into gravel.

If you can picture two rows of prisoners, the one row had prisoners with hammers, the back row had prisoners with no hammers. That was us.

One day the authorities said to us, 'From now on you are doing light prison labour.' They took away our hammers and gave us old prison jerseys and things to mend.

We did not know what was happening. But unknown to us they were taking photographs. We were sitting in the back row of the photo.

We subsequently heard that the photographers had hardly reached the harbour when the jerseys were taken away and the hammers returned. It was intended to show the world that Mandela was doing light prison labour.

Naturally the photograph was not published in South Africa because the law prohibited the papers from publishing anything about prisons or prisoners.

But it was shown internationally; Mandela was doing only light prison labour.

There was no garden at the time. The courtyard was a wasteland, hard, stark and barren.]

08.

"Daylight eases the fears and the perplexities of man, and most often it is like a balm

and a benediction ... there are certain categories of human beings who do not welcome the light of day. A prisoner hugs the night, which is a robe to warm and protect him and comfort him, and daylight brings no cheer to a condemned man. But most often, daylight washes out the confusions of the night."

Howard Fast, *Spartacus*

[08.

At night when you're alone, especially on Robben Island, in your single cells, you have all the time in the world to think about all sorts of things. At night you start worrying. At night you might read your letters from outside, and sometimes you get bad news, and you're alone.

The light was on all the time. Strictly speaking, you were not allowed to cover your head with a blanket, though some did, and you do get used to sleeping with the light on.

You live in a single cell and after lock-up are not allowed to talk.

But you worry about things: you worry about your colleagues, about what's happening to their families. You get only trickles of information. My family was never tormented except for the refusal of passports and so forth, but the families of people like Walter and Madiba were harassed – tortured, jailed, detained. One worried about them, as well.

The night was also a time for private grieving – for Babla; for my mother who died in 1972; for my 'second mother', Mrs Aminabai Pahad (a dedicated fighter against racism herself who virtually adopted me as her own son); for my brother Ismail; and for Dr Dadoo, my leader, my colleague, my father, my older brother, my guide, my mentor, my friend. When Babla's widow, Rookie, visited me in 1984, full of courage, loyalty and the spirit of independence, I was reminded of how many near and dear ones I'd lost in the twenty-one years since losing my freedom. I made a list of them – it came to almost eighty.

But daylight comes and you are together with your comrades and there is no time for fear. You concentrate on different things: your studies, your little bits of news, your conversations. If a comrade is at a low ebb, invariably Walter or somebody would go to him and boost his spirits.]

09.

"There is a great man who makes every man feel small. But the real great man is the man who makes every man feel great."

Dickens

[09.

There are very few adjectives I would not use when speaking about Walter Sisulu.

Prison conditions bring out the best and the worst in human beings. Walter epitomised the very best.

While Madiba was a big brother, Walter was the father. More than that, he was loved by everybody across the political spectrum. Madiba was greatly respected and admired, but not to the extent that Walter was loved. Nobody ever quarrelled with Walter and everybody would go to him with their problems. His care for the welfare of fellow prisoners remained undiminished throughout. He was just a different kind of human being.

He was not educated in the normal sense. He came to jail with only Standard 4, though he did leave with a GCE qualification.

Walter didn't know property – he just didn't understand private possessions. We'd do our washing and hang it up – all of us put our numbers on our clothing. Every now and then someone would say, 'I'm missing jacket number so-and-so.' We'd all chorus, 'It's Walter.' It was true. He'd pick up anything and take it, because he just didn't know.

Michael Dingake (a fellow prisoner who was severely tortured before his incarceration) recalled that the most generous person he knew was Laloo Chiba, who gave everything away, but that there was one more generous than Chiba, and that was Walter. He not only gave his own things away, he also gave away other people's!

09 – Continued

People from the general cells, who somehow smuggled themselves into B section, would go straight to Walter: 'We're short of soap, short of this, and this.' He'd give away everything in his cell. If they were still short he'd come into my cell whether I was there or not. He'd give away my things. Nobody would object because it was Walter.

In my very personal matters I could go to him. Not only could I confide in him but I would listen to his advice. (I was very privileged to be regarded as a member of the Sisulu family and was asked by them to be one of the chairpersons of the massive memorial before Walter's burial.) Madiba, almost until Walter's death, used to consult with him, even when he was president.

As modest and accommodating as Walter was, when it came to matters of principle, especially political principle, he was no pushover. Oh no!]

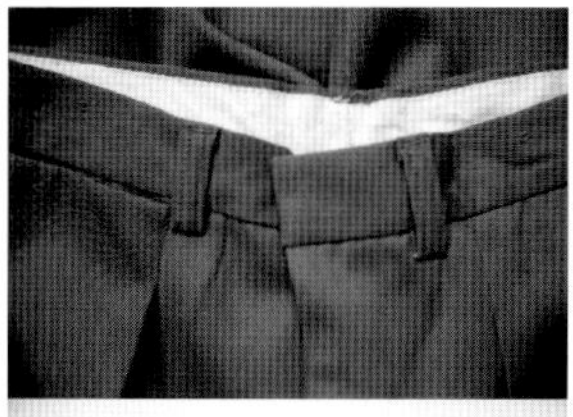

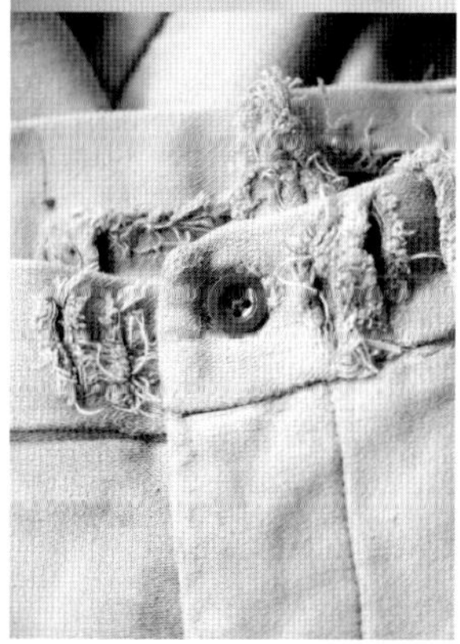

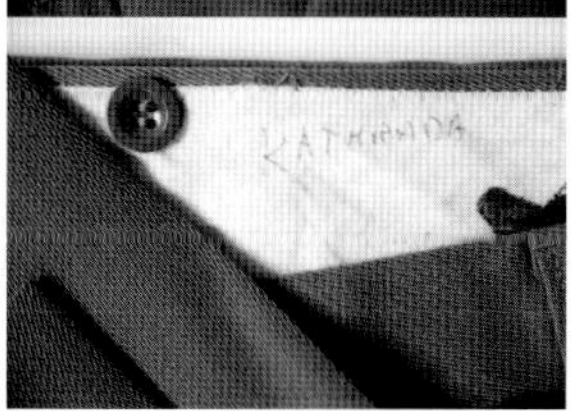

10.

"That song, whose breath
Might lead to death,
But never to retreating."

Sean O'Casey

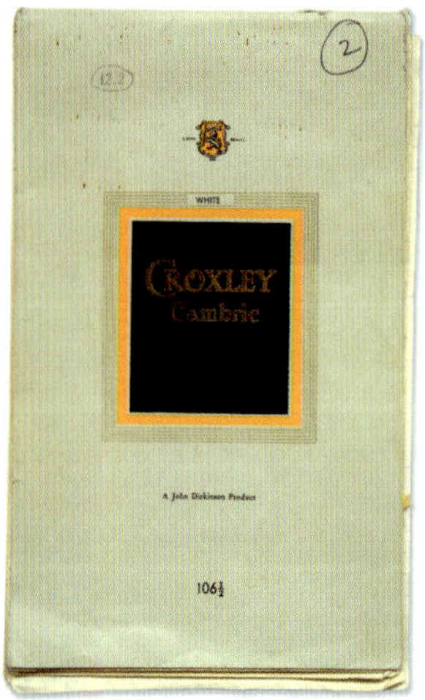

[10.

When, after he was released, Walter was asked what he would have done if he had been sentenced to death, he replied, 'I would have been strong, I would have died singing.'

He then added, 'I would have used a strong voice so people outside could hear it.'

During our ninety-day detention the deadly silence was broken now and again by the sound of struggle songs and the national anthem. We learnt that fellow prisoners sang for us – to encourage us, and to demonstrate solidarity.

On Robben Island, prisoners formed choirs; choirs to sing classical songs, and choirs to sing lighter songs. There were end-of-year concerts where the South African national anthem was sung at each appropriate opportunity. In 'B' section Joshua Zulu (Natal MK member) gave special music classes to those who seriously wished to learn. He had been a music teacher outside. Govan Mbeki and others who had been educated in Mission schools had music as part of their syllabus.]

One may not always find what one looks
if one looks hard enough, one finds something.

—

The greatest derangement of the mind is to believe t
one want to believe them & not because one has see
they are. — Bossuet

Sow flowers, and flowers will blossom
Around you wherever you go;
Sow weeds, and of weeds reap the harvest,
You'll reap whatever you sow.

You'll reap whatever you sow, . . .
The harvest is certainly coming:
You'll reap whatever you sow.

Sow blessings, and blessings will ripen:
Sow hatred, and hatred will grow:
Sow mercy, and reap sweet compassion:
You'll reap whatever you sow.

Sow love, and its sweetness uprising
Shall fill all your heart with its glow;
Sow hope, and receive its fruition:
You'll reap whatsoever you'll sow

— Hymn No 191 Alexander's Hymns

A man lives not only his personal life, as an individu
but also, consciously or unconsciously, the life of his epoch an
his contemporaries

"Time has no divisions to mark its passage, there is nev
blare of trumpets to announce the b

11.

"God had infinite time to give us;

but how did He give it? In one immense tract of lazy millenniums? No, He cut it up into a neat succession of new mornings."

Ralph Waldo Emerson

[11.

To survive in prison what you have to do is change the environment, as far as possible, into a normal society. The moment you enter prison you have to stamp your dignity. You don't allow these chaps to humiliate you. Once you allow them to impinge on your dignity, they will continue to do that for the rest of your prison life.

To turn your mind away from the slow passing of time, and to make life less intolerable, you have to try to normalise your surroundings. I accepted that, do what I would, or could, there was no way in which I was going to shorten my life imprisonment. Therefore my cell was going to be my home for years and years. And I knew that I was going to spend hours of each working day in my cell. And weekends and rainy days would lengthen the time. Therefore, in the interest of my health, and to adjust to the reality of having to spend this inordinate amount of time in my little home, I had to make it pleasing to the eye. I wasn't allowed to change the drab prison-grey colour of the walls, but I could, without specific permission, introduce some colour, however little. So in my stationery order I put down rolls of colourful gift-wrap, ostensibly to cover my books. But I used it to cover the three metal lockers on the wall, and my bookcase. And as we were allowed more photographs, instead of putting them all in the album, I placed some on the bookcase.

Once again, there's regulations. Regulations allowed you to buy soap, toothpaste, shaving cream, blades. These were absolute necessities. In my case, whenever I got a chance I ordered things with nothing specific in mind – just with the idea that some day we might need to use them. So I ordered parchment, glue, mapping pens, rice paper. And, when we had to smuggle out the Mandela biography, the parchment was used to cover the makeshift album – constructed by Laloo Chiba – the glue was used to seal it and the mapping pens were used by Chiba and another 'B' section comrade Mac Maharaj to transcribe Madiba's manuscript in tiny handwriting on to rice paper. The album containing large maps was so expertly assembled that it looked as if it was factory-made. Mac Maharaj was to be released in 1976; his task was to take out the album, which he did easily and without causing any suspicion. As planned, he sent it to London, where it eventually became the bestseller *Long Walk to Freedom*.

So those things I collected seemingly so irrelevant ... it's humble things that sometimes carry the great.]

12.

"The earth hears me.

The sun hears me.
Shall I lie?"

Form of oath-taking among Shoshone Indians

[12.

Early in 1965 we started work at the lime quarry. Pick and shovels. It was very difficult – bleeding hands, blisters, Mercurochrome balm – none of us had ever done this kind of work in our lives. But there were advantages. We could talk, we could work in groups. We could study. We could disseminate news – smuggled, as well as whatever bits had been gathered from visits and letters. Naturally you couldn't use pen and paper, or books. But we had the advantage of comrades who had been teachers outside, and other educated people. We were able to have classes and discussions with them. Neville Alexander (who held a doctorate in German literature and a History degree), Les van der Heyden (a secondary-school teacher), Mandla Masondo (a lecturer in Mathematics), to name but a few ... After a few months the blisters disappeared and our hands stopped bleeding.

We continued to assert the stand that we had taken right at the beginning – we would work as much as we were able to – we would not be forced into doing more. At all times we would jealously guard our dignity.

It was tough. There were very hard patches, like stone, or a little less hard than stone, that we had to break through. We would pile the lime into heaps, which we would then shovel onto lorries. The lime would be mixed with crushed seashells, and used for the roads. They could have used machines if they really wanted large quantities of lime, but we were sentenced to be punished, and hard labour was part of our punishment.

We were at the quarry for thirteen years. But it wasn't always uphill. There were times of relaxation when we did little or, at times, no work. Warders who were on guard on the bank above would whistle when they saw an officer's vehicle approach, and we would start work again. It fluctuated. At one stage we smuggled in a radio but after it ran out of batteries and was too dangerous to keep we buried it in the quarry.

We must always remember that the conditions in the communal sections were vastly different. In 'B' section we were only thirty; the communal cells had hundreds and hundreds of inmates. They worked at the stone quarry, and they were continually punished for allegedly not working hard enough. Some landed in hospital during a hunger strike when they were too weak to work.

With all the disadvantages of the winter cold, the glare of the sun, the lime dust, and pick and shovel work, most of us still preferred to go to the quarry. It was good to be outside the cell, and out in the open. When we had to remain in the section to see the doctor, we were frequently kept locked up, not always with our books in our own cell, but in an empty cell. This too was part of the punishment, because 'you didn't come to jail to read books ...'

However, there was one casualty of the lime quarry – Madiba. The glare of the sun and the lime dust affected his eyes. Which is why, if you want to take a photo of him or with him, you will be asked not to use a flash camera.]

"Time seems to change its nature

in prison. The present hardly exists for there is an absence of feeling and sensation which might separate it from the dead past. Even news of the active, living and dying world outside has a certain dreamlike unreality, an immobility and an unchangeableness as of the past. The outer objective time ceases to be, the inner and subjective sense remains but at a lower level, except when thought pulls it out of the present and experiences a kind of reality in the past or in the future. We live, as Auguste Comte said, dead men's lives, encased in our pasts, but this is especially so in prison when we try to find some sustenance for our starved and locked-up emotions in memory of the past or fancies of the future.

There is a stillness and everlastingness about the past. It changes not and has a touch of eternity, like a painted picture or a statue in bronze or marble. Unaffected by the storms and upheavals of the present, it maintains its dignity and repose and tempts the troubled spirit and the tortured mind to seek shelter in its vaulted catacombs. There is peace there and security, and one may even sense a spiritual quality.

But it is not life, unless we can find the vital links between it and the present with all its conflicts and problems. It is a kind of art for art's sake without the passion and the urge to action which are the very stuff of life. Without that passion and urge, there is a gradual oozing out of hope and vitality, a settling down on lower levels of existence, a slow merging into nonexistence. We become prisoners of the past and some part of its immobility sticks to us. The passage of the mind is all the easier in prison where action is denied and we become slaves to the routine of jail life.

Yet the past is ever with us and all that we are and all that we have comes from the past. We are its products and we live immersed in it. Not to understand it and feel it as something living within us is not to understand the present. To combine it with the present and extend it to the future, to break from it where it cannot be so united, to make of all this the pulsating and vibrating material for thought and action – that is life."

Nehru, *The Discovery of India*

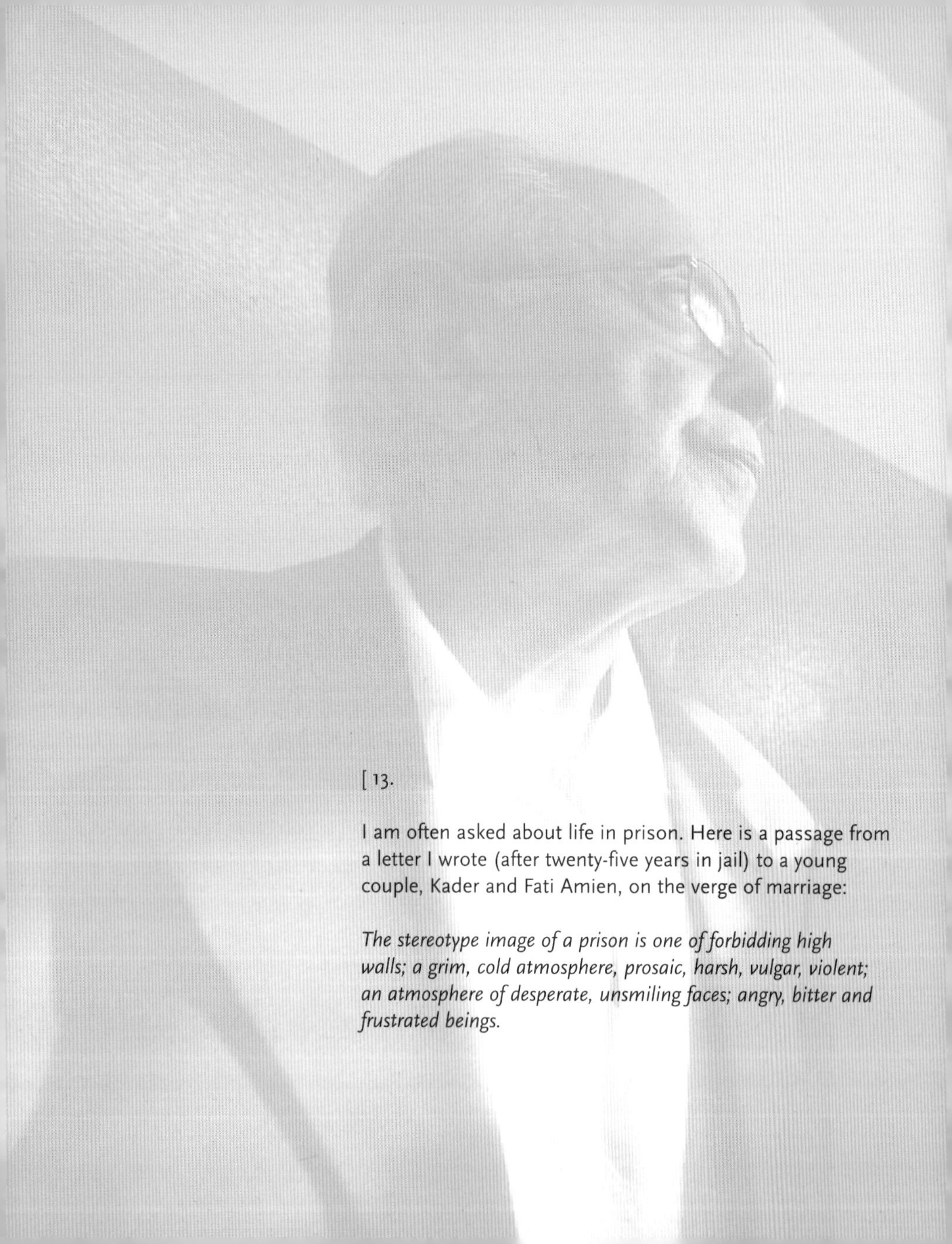

[13.

I am often asked about life in prison. Here is a passage from a letter I wrote (after twenty-five years in jail) to a young couple, Kader and Fati Amien, on the verge of marriage:

The stereotype image of a prison is one of forbidding high walls; a grim, cold atmosphere, prosaic, harsh, vulgar, violent; an atmosphere of desperate, unsmiling faces; angry, bitter and frustrated beings.

Admittedly, a prison situation is tailor-made for the projection of such an image ... It is easy to succumb when faced with prospects of a lengthy and nightmarish existence and consequently dwell on one's miseries, hardships, the manifold deprivations and negative experiences. Someone has written about two prisoners looking out of their cell window – the one saw iron bars while the other saw stars. How true!

Naturally one does not uncomplainingly accept all the wrongs and hope for the best. No, but one has to accept that there are certain realities over which one has no control. For example, the very fact of being in prison means that one has to endure certain deprivations, the chief of which is the loss of one's freedom. Secondly, one is thrust into a community in which you have no say as to who your fellow inmates should be. Having come to terms with these and similar unchangeables, you immediately set about the task of adapting yourself to the new environment and where necessary and possible you immerse yourself in the intolerable. In the process, brick by brick, you are building up the other – and certainly in the case of security prisoners, the real – picture of prison life. It is a picture of great warmth, fellowship, friendship, humour and laughter; of strong convictions, of a generosity of spirit, of compassion, solidarity and care. It is a picture of continuous learning, of getting to know and live with your fellow beings, their strengths as well as their idiosyncrasies; but more important, where one comes to know oneself, one's weaknesses, inadequacies and one's potentials. Unbelievably, it is a very positive, confident, determined – yes, even a happy community ...

To move away from a self-centred lifestyle to one where the individual personality is largely submerged in a wider social unit is a profoundly humbling, but enormously rewarding experience.]

"No one knows what kind of government it is who has never been in prison."

Tolstoy

❄

"In order to become a dragon, a chameleon must pass a very vigorous examination."

Chinese proverb

❄

[14.

We were locked up each afternoon between 4.30 and five, until 5.30 the next morning. We came back from work about four, showered, washed, and then took our food into our cells. Strictly speaking we should have been eating outside, or in the dining hall, but the warders essentially were also workers, and didn't want to work a minute after hours. If they had to knock off at 4.30, they would knock off, regardless. This often worked to our advantage.

At weekends, from Friday to Monday, we were locked up all

the time except for an hour on Saturday and an hour on Sunday, when we were brought out of the cell, to walk in the courtyard.

There were some ridiculous regulations. Being a maximum-security prison, the lights remained on all night. In order to register for studies with a correspondence college or the University of South Africa we had to get formal permission, and only people who received funds from their *immediate* family were given permission. Now, if you were studying Standard 8 you had to sleep at eight o'clock, lights on; Standard 10, you slept at ten; university, you slept at eleven. A warder would patrol the passage the whole night; anyone caught with a book or pen and paper after these hours was punished, generally by deprivation of food.

The warders who worked physically close to us were not armed. The quarry warders were also unarmed, except for those who stood right on top.

At the beginning, when we had to be brought out to the courtyard during exercise time, this could only be done if there was an armed warder on the overlooking catwalk. As time went by, this would be relaxed, and eventually it was discontinued. But the four tall watch towers on each corner of the prison complex were continuously manned by an armed guard, twenty-four hours a day.

With gradual relaxation, the brutality in the communal cells had more or less come to a stop. We in 'B' section never experienced physical violence and, in about 1978, there were some significant improvements. A relatively enlightened officer allowed us to switch off the lights at night; all prisoners were given beds; and censored radio news bulletins were piped into the different prison sections. In 1980 we were also allowed newspapers.]

15.

"I grumbled because I had no shoes until I met a man who had no feet."

Chinese proverb

[15.

Among the most welcome diversions that helped to break the monotony of jail life were the visits of clergy persons. Encouraged by Madiba and Walter, a number of us regularly attended all the services – Christian, Muslim, Hindu. Our congregations were made up of believers, but we also attended out of respect and gratitude.

On cold or hot Sundays, during calm or stormy seas, these men of the cloth would come. We appreciated their concern, understanding, and especially their empathy. They were a constant source of encouragement and comfort. However, we must confess that, among some of us, there was the additional element of self-interest. It was a desire to be out of our cells and in the courtyard, especially in the sunshine. But the clergymen were also our contact with civilian life outside prison. Some, albeit to a very limited extent, were a source of news. In one instance two of our comrades, Eddie Daniels and Hennie Ferris, actually managed to steal the *Sunday Times* from the bag of Brother September! While Mr

Govender helped to enrich our garden by bringing chilli and tomato seeds, Imam Bassier brought us news of community life in Cape Town; and on one occasion, through him, I managed to smuggle out a message of our hunger strike. A zealous warder once observed the eagerness with which some of our comrades lined up for Holy Communion. This resulted in the prohibition of communion wine! I don't know if the orange juice substitute met with the biblical requirements, but needless to say the number of congregants for Holy Communion declined dramatically.

In particular though there was an old Anglican clergyman – such a wonderful man. Very naive at times, too, but we knew one thing, his sympathy was with us. Not necessarily because he agreed with our politics but just because he was a kind and concerned human being. Everybody loved Father Hughes. Even after all the time he spent with us, sometimes he would still mistake another prisoner, Fikile Bam, for Madiba – and would take him aside and kindly talk to him about his wife Winnie and how she was getting on.

Once during his sermon he quoted this proverb to us, and it has stuck in my mind ever since. In fact even now when people ask me how we endured hardship for so many years, I quote this proverb; explaining that it may have been hard for us, but what about our comrades in the same struggle who were having it much worse. The tortured, the assassinated, the harassed, the hanged. We were protected. We had no fears about a policeman coming to Robben Island and shooting at us. The killings of our comrades were carried out, not by warders on Robben Island, but by police. Outside. (During the Soweto uprising of 1976, an estimated six hundred schoolchildren were killed by the police.) That knowledge was always there. It still is.]

"Bread has no sorrow for me, and water no affliction.

But to shut me from the light of the sky, and the sight of the fields and flowers; to chain my feet so that I can never again ride with the soldiers nor climb the hills; to make me breathe foul damp darkness, and keep from me everything that brings me back to the love of God when your wickedness and foolishness tempt me to hate Him: all this is worse than the furnace in the Bible that was heated seven times. I could do without my war horse; I could drag about in a skirt; I could let the banners and the trumpets and the knights and soldiers pass me and leave me behind as they leave the other women, if only I could still hear the wind in the trees, the larks in the sunshine, the young lambs crying through the healthy frost, and the blessed, blessed church bells that send my angel voices floating to me on the wind.

But without these things I cannot live; and by your wanting to take them away from me, or from any human creature, I know that your counsel is of the devil, and that mine is of God."

George Bernard Shaw, *Saint Joan*

[16.

Since my youth I have read, or come across, reports about unbelievable atrocities committed by man against his fellow human beings. I knew a little about Joan of Arc, about the Inquisition, and during the war about the atrocities in Nazi concentration camps. Not long after that the little girl Anne Frank's diary shocked the world.

In 1951 I had visited Prague where Gestapo chief Gauleiter Reinhard Heydrich had been assassinated. The Nazis accused the villagers of Lidice of hiding his assassins and shot every male inhabitant and destroyed the village. When I visited it, Lidice had been rebuilt but it was a village of widows and children.

At Auschwitz extermination camp I looked into the heart of darkness of humanity – the trench in which dogs savaged people to death, the gas chambers, the incinerators, the pillows made of human hair and the lampshades of human skin. The streets outside the crematoria were littered with small pieces of human bones. I brought back a handful of bones with me to South Africa to remind our people of the outcome of racism.

St Joan articulated, much better than I could, what confinement meant. It was as if she was talking about us. Now, when I read the words 'bread', 'water', 'chains', I think of Robben Island.

We could never compare our suffering with hers. But she was speaking for us.

I certainly did like nature, having been born and brought up in the countryside, so when it rained on Robben Island and we got the smell of the rain, it brought that childhood back to me, brought Schweizer-Reneke back to me. Almost every evening, after lock up, the animals used to gather outside. Since my cell faced the sea I could get onto my chair and through the window watch them coming, the ostriches, the buck, the guinea fowl, the partridges, and the noisy and selfish seagulls

We did not realise how much we would miss the rainbow. When we did see one we just stared at it because we had not seen one for ages. A few times, while working at the quarry, it made an appearance. And that image sticks.]

“As good almost kill a man as kill a good book. Who kills a man kills a reasonable creature, God’s image, but he who destroys a good book, kills reason itself, kills the image of God, as it were, in the eye. Many a man lives a burden to the earth; but a good book is the precious lifeblood of a master spirit, embalmed and treasured up on purpose to a life beyond life.”

Milton

[17.

Riffling through the quotations I kept (illegally) in jail it surprises me the number and titles of books that were in our libraries, and those we managed to smuggle in.

Robben Island prison consisted of three sections, completely isolated from one another. There were libraries in each section, each with their own librarian. I was librarian in ‘B’ section, and our library was housed in what was supposed to be the storeroom.

A lot of the titles made no sense to the warders, so they just satisfied their own arbitrary criteria when it came to censorship. As far as they were concerned, they were looking for the words 'communist', 'Mandela', 'ANC', 'PAC' (the Pan African Congress – a breakaway liberation movement from the ANC). The rest, they allowed.

My being a librarian offered certain advantages for our political work. In order to preserve this position I specially did the degree Bachelor of Bibliography, for which Library Science was a major. My second major, African Politics, allowed me to order books which otherwise we would not be able to get.

There were other advantages. I was heading the ANC's communications committee (also illegal), whose task included establishing and keeping contact with our comrades in the other sections. The librarians in the other sections were also ANC members. We looked forward to the annual stocktaking, when we three were brought together to count the books in each section. Virtually unsupervised, we deliberately spent more days than required to count the measly few thousand books.

When Tokyo Sexwale and other post-Soweto uprising leaders arrived on Robben Island they were put in a different section which had no library, so each week I was allowed to take them a catalogue and deliver their orders. In this way we got the first comprehensive report of the 1976 uprising of the school-children in Soweto, and the subsequent massacre.

Whenever we managed to acquire newspapers, either from the rubbish dump, or from bribing a warder, the loot came to me to go through and then distribute clippings to a handful of comrades for dissemination by word of mouth. I took every opportunity to devour anything and everything of interest. In the process I became a hopeless addict. It is eighteen years since my release, and I simply cannot get rid of the habit. I can't just skim for what is important. I waste a lot of time reading every item of a newspaper. And on Sundays I get five of them.]

18.

"We can forgive cruelty –

to wound a person means that one still has faith in him – but not indifference. Indifference is like ice at the poles, it deadens everything."

Balzac, *Lost Illusions*

[18.

My first degree in jail was a BA with majors in History and Criminology. I received permission to study late in 1964, and therefore only registered in 1965.

There was a debate among us because the regulations said we would be allowed to do only one degree, and no more. Where my comrades said, 'Let us stagger the thing and keep on studying for a longer time,' I disagreed, saying, 'No, let's finish, and then fight for more.' And that's what I did. I was the first one to finish (in 1968). Of course, there were a number of comrades who had degrees before they came to prison.

In 1968 they said, 'You've finished.' I said, 'No, I'm doing a life sentence, and I can't spend the years doing nothing.' After a lot of debate they conceded, but only partially. They said, 'OK, we'll allow you to do some subjects for non-degree purposes.' I spent some years doing Anthropology, Ancient History, and things like that. But I kept on fighting to be allowed to do Honours. After a while they said, 'We won't allow you to do Honours, but we'll allow you to do another bachelor's degree.' So I chose to do a B.Bibliography, a four-year course, with majors in Library Science and African Politics.

After I finished the second degree, it was once again a repetition of the previous fight. Eventually they said, 'Alright, we'll allow you to do Honours, but only one.' I completed BA Honours in History, and, déjà vu, I was then allowed to do Honours in African Politics. By then I was in Pollsmoor and I decided to resort to legal action to be allowed to do a masters degree but the legal process was deliberately strung out – on a decision taken by the United Democratic Front (UDF) comrades outside – so that my lawyer, Dullah Omar, one of the leaders of the movement, could 'consult' me about issues other than academic studies. It was an exciting time in politics.

The matter dragged on for about a year, during which time there was a continuous exchange of affidavits between the lawyers on both sides. With chief warder Christo Brand turning a blind eye, Dullah brought in his bag not legal books but delicious home-cooked food from his wife, Farieda, and others.

Eventually the authorities conceded and said I could do a masters, even a doctorate.

But, where the Nationalists failed to stop me studying, something just as insidious did. We were allowed television, and in our cell Walter and I revelled in it, and out of the (barred) window went my studies. Thanks to the courage and compassion of Christo Brand, we smuggled in videos banned in the rest of South Africa!]

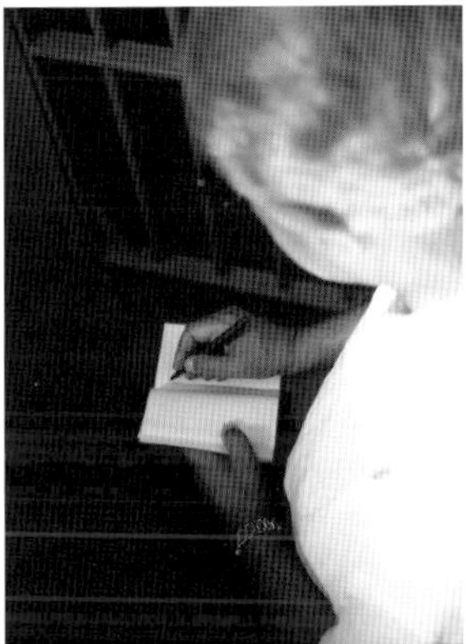

19.

"The Lord did not create woman from man's head, so that he can

command her; nor from man's foot, so that she would be his slave. God made Eve from Adam's side so that woman will always be nearest to man's heart … Be careful not to make a woman weep: God counts her tears."

The *Talmud*

[19.

As things relaxed, at the end of each year we were allowed to organise sports tournaments, poetry readings, singing, and choir performances. We were also allowed to purchase goodies such as chocolates, biscuits and dried fruit. In addition, at Christmas time our African comrades were allowed to purchase one loaf of bread!

At one of the end-of-year concerts we put on the play *Antigone,* by the modern playwright, Anouilh.

Why *Antigone?*

Because its fundamental message was that, in the face of a death sentence, Antigone stood up against her father's unjust and cruel treatment of her brother. That's the message that impressed me and the other comrades. She was the obvious choice.

Like Antigone, Anne Frank represented courage. We managed to smuggle her *Diary* in, and it made a huge impact. I'm sure we passed it on to our comrades in the communal cells, too.

In some ways her situation was similar to ours. But, of course, hers was much worse. Like Antigone and St Joan, she faced certain death. We admired the courage and maturity of this young girl, as well as the heroism of the Dutch family who harboured the Franks at extreme risk to themselves.

In *Antigone,* the part of her father, Creon, was played by Madiba!]

“If we work upon marble,

it will perish;
If we work upon brass, time will efface it;
If we rear temples, they will crumble into dust;
But if we work upon immortal minds,
If we imbue them with principles,
With the just fear of God and love of our fellow men,
We engrave upon those tablets something
which will brighten to all eternity.”

Daniel Webster

[20.

There was always stimulation. Every now and then a new prisoner would come in, and we got information about matters like what was happening in liberation organisations – information we couldn't get from newspapers.

For all members of the ANC we had a political syllabus, which every one of us, every new arrival, had to go through.

Walter Sisulu was first up, the expert on the history of the ANC. Other members conducted classes on different topics, of a political, social and economic nature. Then we had all sorts of polemics, discussions and debates; one such was on circumcision. Some of our chaps from the communal cells who worked in the prison hospital managed to set up a clandestine circumcision school.

A serious debate resurfaced with the arrival of young MK cadres who had received their military training in the Soviet Union and other communist countries. They maintained that we had been too long in prison, and were ignorant of the latest policy developments in the ANC. In essence, their view was that there had been a radical change in the direction of our struggle. From the original aim for a national or bourgeois democracy, the struggle was now for the attainment of a 'people's democracy'. We thought that the debate had been settled by the time we were transferred to Pollsmoor. But not so. In fact, shades of the debate still continue today, and it seems likely to go on forever.

There was also the occasional frivolous discussion. One that went on for a long time was a debate about whether there were tigers in Africa. One chap maintained that the African languages did not strictly differentiate between the different members of the cat family. I don't think we ever reached finality on this topic.

While these polemics did help to while away the time, we cannot deny that by and large they also helped to broaden our knowledge. ∣

21.

“One writes of scars healed,

a loose parallel to the pathology of the skin, but there is no such thing in the life of an individual. There are open wounds, shrunk sometimes to the size of a pinprick, but wounds still.”

F Scott Fitzgerald, *Tender is the Night*

[21.

The warders used to beat up prisoners with batons and rubber truncheons. There is a common term called a 'carry-on'; it is only used in prisons. A carry-on is when a mass of armed warders systematically, indiscriminately, and repeatedly carry out assaults on a mass of prisoners. It is not an individual beating.

Our comrades in the communal cells were frequently victims of carry-ons, together with common-law prisoners. However, for reasons of their own, the warders never used physical violence against us in 'B' section.

While we escaped physical violence we came very close to it. It was on the night of Friday, 28 May 1971 – which I regard as the very worst night of my twenty-six years in prison. A night that will never be erased from my memory. It was bitterly cold, the beginning of winter. We had already been locked up. Some of us had gone to sleep, some were busy with their studies

We suddenly heard the doors and grilles being unlocked, and we were invaded by a horde of drunken warders under the command of the sadist, Lieutenant Fourie. They had just come from a brutal carry-on in the criminal prison (by this stage the criminal and political prisoners had been separated), where they had mercilessly beaten up people, leaving behind broken bones, head injuries, weals and bruises.

In that mood, still fresh, they entered our cells, ordered us to strip completely naked, and face the wall with our arms outstretched against it. They were ostensibly searching for newspapers and other contraband. In fact, we were being punished because we had, in solidarity, joined our Namibian comrades on a hunger strike and they hoped to break it.

Fortunately, our discipline was what saved us from incalculable physical injury and bloodshed. One false move on our part would have resulted in just that. In their drunken fury they could even have killed some of us. It was frightening; more than that it was utterly humiliating and disgraceful.

While we were still enduring the cold against the wall, Govan Mbeki collapsed. The assailants panicked. We panicked too. We thought it was a heart attack. Fortunately it wasn't; it was stress. And when that happened they said, 'OK, you can dress up.'

But they had not completely satisfied their thirst for blood. So they turned the corner into the central wing, where Andimba Toivo ya Toivo (one of our Namibian comrades) was kept in isolation, together with a few comrades from the communal cells who were being punished for some transgression. They went into Andimba's cell and assaulted him, but he retaliated by knocking one of them down. (This was to earn him nine months solitary confinement.)

The next day Eddie Daniels had a visit from his brother. When Eddie tried to tell him of the assaults, and to report the matter to lawyers, the visit was summarily cut short.

Luckily we survived to tell the story.]

22.

"The best thing to give to your enemy is forgiveness;

to an opponent, tolerance; to a friend, your ear; to your child, good example; to your father, reverence; to your mother, conduct that will make her proud of you; to yourself, respect; to all men, charity."

Benjamin Franklin

[22.

It may seem strange that I have returned countless times to the island where we endured so much, but I can because, with the help of my comrades, I survived it, I learned from it and, in the process and in the end, transcended it.

Today, twenty-six years later, if in my mind I try to re-enact the night of Friday, 28 May 1971, I find myself overcome with one and only one emotion – HATRED! Hatred for the humiliation they inflicted on me, and especially on my elders and leaders. But then comes Saturday and Sunday, and the days, weeks and months that follow. The scars of humiliation remain; they cannot go away. Indeed they should not go away. It is our history. Lest we forget. But the erstwhile emotion of hatred dissipates and weakens. Its place is taken by reason and a clearer mind. I question myself. Did Chief Luthuli (president of the ANC), Dr Dadoo and Bram Fischer (Rivonia Trial defence lawyer who was later also sentenced to life imprisonment) not teach me that hate, like bitterness and revenge, is a negative emotion? Piet Fourie and his brutal warders were mere cogs in the racial machine of apartheid. They were characters who should be looked upon with pity, not hate. When the dust of conflict and struggle and blood-shed settled they were still going to be with us. They, and those who were guilty of indoctrinating them to believe that we were inferior beings, could not be drowned in the sea. We were going to strive to win them over and join in the building of a new, non-racial, democratic South Africa. Hate must give way to FORGIVENESS and RECONCILIATION. There is no other way.]

23.

"He drew a circle to shut me out –
Heretic, rebel, a thing to flout.
But Love and I had the wit to win;
We drew a circle that took him in."

Edwin Markham, 'The Spirit of Magnanimity'

[23.

The ANC always considered itself a broad church which embraced everybody – communists, anti-communists, capitalists, socialists, anti-capitalists, everybody – drawing them in, instead of leaving them out. You had your conservatives, you had your radicals, but for everybody there was a place. (When Madiba became president, he even tried to make room for the PAC to be part of the government, despite it not having the required percentage of votes in the 1994 election.)

Eddie Daniels was the only member of the Liberal Party on Robben Island; he belonged to its members who had formed an armed group – the Armed Resistance Movement.

The parents of some of the younger members who were on trial and sentenced with him made representations to the Minister of Justice, B J Vorster, and they were released before completing their sentences. Without Eddie's knowledge a visiting judge made similar representations to the government to release him. They were prepared to do so provided he gave certain undertakings. Eddie refused, and served his full fifteen years. There were elements in prison who wanted to isolate Eddie because 'he was a Liberal'. That wasn't ANC policy. Whatever our differences may have been with the Liberal Party, here was a man who was serving fifteen years in the struggle against apartheid, and we were never going to isolate him.

On one occasion we were having a memorial meeting for one of the senior ANC leaders, Moses Kotane, who had passed away in exile. The same elements conveyed to us that they would not attend if Eddie was among the speakers. Our response was that Eddie had been on Robben Island with us for many years, and he was our comrade. We would not exclude Eddie. So they stayed away; the memorial went ahead without them.

I've been privileged to know Eddie. He and I remain close friends.]

“Miss Maud said:

‘Your father’s right. Mockingbirds don’t do one thing but make music for us to enjoy. They don’t eat up people’s gardens, don’t nest in corncribs, they don’t do one thing but sing their hearts out for us. That’s why it’s a sin to kill a mockingbird.’”

Harper Lee, *To Kill a Mockingbird*

[24.

What was the worst deprivation? Well, naturally, freedom of movement is a major deprivation, but when I’m asked the question over and over again, especially when I accompany people to the island, I always answer that the greatest was the absence of children.

Prison is an unnatural society. So one even looks forward to hearing a child crying, just to hear its voice, even from a distance; and, of course, a child’s laughter.

In our case, children were deliberately kept away from us. When I stood on my chair and looked out of the window,

I used to wait for any length of time just to have a fleeting look at the children of warders walking towards the harbour with their parents.

I can never ever forget the day in 1983 when for the first time in twenty years I held a child in my arms, and kissed and cuddled her! And that was by accident. Three-year-old Priya accompanied her lawyer-father when he had come to see me, and she wouldn't wait alone in the car. The warders relented and allowed her to come in. My mind was in a whirl; on my way back to the cell I almost had to pinch myself to confirm that I had actually held a child on my lap. For those few glorious moments I just held her, and kept stroking her long hair.

Two-year-old Shameez (the daughter of friends) was allowed to visit with her father and mother, but I couldn't touch her. She looked at me through the glass that separated us, and suddenly said, 'I don't like police!' What a thrill. But alas, only momentary. Later she looked at me, and said, 'I don't like you!'

Then a few years later there came another friend's child, Nadia – extrovert, self-confident, no respecter of iron bars, uniforms, regulations. She walked freely about like an old hand. She danced for me, and just a few moments after her performance she was in my arms, chattering away.

These kids made an everlasting impact on me, so much so that I still keep in touch with them. I send birthday cards – I have attended the weddings of two of them. The bond is unbreakable.]

"Often it is a clock, for a clock is not a dead thing,

it recollects the past, it has been ticking through the past, it is ticking now and looks forward to times ahead. A clock lives in the present but it lives in the past and in the future too. It is the ideal present, for it has the freedom of Time's three dimensions."

L P Hartley, *The Betrayal*

[25.

We were never allowed to have watches until about 1985 or 1986, in Pollsmoor. Then they said we were allowed to keep watches, we were allowed to keep pets, we were allowed to have children visiting us. In any repressive society this was revolutionary stuff. The most welcome was to be able to see children. But pets, no. I was adamant. We were in prison, caged in; under no circumstances was I going to imprison a bird in a cage, or fish in a tank. One day a warder's pet parrot flew into our cell at Pollsmoor. We enjoyed witnessing its freedom. It even perched itself on my shoulder while I was at my desk. It was wonderful.

On Robben Island, especially at work, and during exercise time, the warders used to turn their watches to the other side so we couldn't see the time of day. It was a method of curtailing our exercise time, or making time drag on at work. At the quarry we learnt to guess the time by the shadow of the sun; just as we managed to forecast rain by looking at the clouds over Table Mountain.

At some stage on Robben Island, they did allow those of us who were registered students to buy clocks. But no watches at work.

From about 1978 we were no longer taken out to work. We stayed in the section, not always locked in our cells. We could study, and we could play games, or simply walk about in the courtyard. First they said we could only play over weekends, but that didn't last. They even allowed us to buy track suits; at first only to wear at weekends, but later, whenever we felt like it.

You know, there is no logic or reason in prison. There are only regulations to regiment your life. Regulations in place of hearts, regulations in place of discretion. At the time when regulations had stipulated short trousers for Africans throughout the year, summer and winter, some of us (Indians and coloureds) wanted to wear short trousers in summer, especially at the quarry. 'No,' they said. 'Regulations say you have to wear long trousers.' So we suffered in the heat.]

"Huck to Tom, complaining about life

at the home of puritanical Widow Douglas: 'I've tried it, and it don't work; it don't work, Tom. It ain't for me … The widder eats by a bell; she goes to bed by a bell; she gets up by a bell – everything's so awful reg'lar a body can't stand it.'"

Mark Twain, *The Adventures of Tom Sawyer*

[26.

Huck Finn wasn't in prison, but everything else about his sentiments reminded us of our situation. Everything was done by the bell.

First of all, the bell rings and you've got to get up. Either the bell rings, or we are commanded, 'Get ready for inspection.' So we stand at the door of our cells, until the officer passes. After we've finished breakfast the bell rings again to tell us we've got to line up to go to work.

When it's lunch time the bell rings, and again when lunch is over. This, of course, was much more rigidly the practice in the communal cells, where the bell's message had to be heard by the hundreds of prisoners. But among the thirty-odd in 'B' section, even when orders were shouted out, the bell remained in our minds. We were, in effect, answering to the bell.

I think why we liked Huck so much was because he was saying, 'I resist the bell, it curbs my freedom.'

More than most of us, Walter could identify with Huck, especially in so far as the bell was concerned. His cell was diagonally opposite mine, and I could witness his habits. The bell would ring, but he wouldn't immediately get out of bed. He'd even perfected a method of sitting up in bed and shaving! The bell we were answering to was: line up, go to work, finish, line up for food ... lock-up time; and Walter was the slowest to come in from the courtyard – he was going to enjoy every last bit of sun in the open, in 'freedom'.

As in his political decision-making, so in his daily life in jail, nothing was going to rush Walter. He would do his thing, patiently and calmly.

Huck and Walter! Who would have ever thought of similarities between the two! But here they were – both rebels against rigidity.]

27.

"I found this (one letter and one visit every six months) the most

inhumane restriction of the prison system. Communication with one's family is a human right. In prison, the only thing worse than bad news about one's family is no news at all … A letter with ill tidings was always preferable to no letter at all … When letters did arrive, they were cherished …"

Nelson Mandela, *Long Walk to Freedom*

[27.

The censors' office was by far the most important office in prison. It was also the most powerful in that we prisoners were dependent on it for physical and written contact with the outside world, especially with our families. There are three people in prison who can make life more or less tolerable: the official who is in charge of the section; the official who is in charge at work; and the censor.

The censors had the power to inflict not physical but emotional pain. And they consistently used that power. They controlled the letters; they decided who was, and who was not allowed to visit; they closely supervised each visit, and they could, and did, summarily terminate those visits before the allotted time of half-an-hour.

At the beginning we were allowed to receive one visit, and write and receive one letter every six months. And the letter had to be restricted to five hundred words. A nasty censor would count the five hundred words, and cut the rest with scissors.

At first, they used to black out what they didn't like. But after complaints they used to underline the objectionable parts, and ask us to rewrite or omit them. Incoming letters continued to be blacked out, or cut with scissors.

There were some nasty censors, and some less nasty. It is not good taste to pursue one who is dead, so I will not talk about a particularly bad one, save to say that, behind his suave exterior, he worked directly with the security police, and behaved like one of them.

27 – Continued

The censors were not allowed to interact with us. They themselves spied on each other, noting which censor might be unnecessarily conversing with a prisoner. Such a report to a higher officer might gain a promotion.

But that is the nature of censorship and the prison system. Like starved dogs in a small cage they turned on each other. That is one of the dangers and one of the evils of censorship.

The censors were aware of the most intimate information about each prisoner. In some instances they were known to abuse this knowledge, and maliciously cause marital problems. The censors were the curse of our lives.]

My Dear Ayesha,

It is such a long time that

you. Uncle Amien told me that

had gone much worse. I

anything at all be done

"In the crises of life, when we are overwhelmed by joy or sorrow

we see our surroundings with sharpened senses, and they remain forever afterwards indelibly part of our experience."

Balzac, *Eugénie Grandet*

[28.

Freedom for some meant sadness for others. This was a letter I wrote when Eddie Daniels was released in 1979.

I'm writing this in the early hours of the morning. It is so quiet except for the rhythmic sound of the waves breaking against the shore as if they were keeping time with the equally rhythmic whistling of the wind. The birds and the crickets and the mosquitoes are all silent. There is not even a stir or a snore from my neighbours. It's as if I'm alone on the island. One feels almost driven towards 'sessions of sweet, silent thoughts and remembrances of things past'. It seems so incongruous to be concerning oneself with mundane things instead of just lying in bed and enjoying the silence and just thinking. If only one were endowed with the talents of a musician, a poet, a writer – any creative artist – then surely this would be the ideal atmosphere.

A door has just banged, a vehicle has come to a screeching stop. And with that we come back to reality. A solitary bird has begun to sing. Soon it will be joined by others. And it will be dawn. That means I better hurry in order to get this away. I've been wondering why I had to choose this moment to write about the wind and the sea and the birds. Is it some form of escapism? Yes, I think it is. Yesterday a very dear friend was released from jail after 15 years! I suppose I wanted to avoid thinking about the vacuum this has created. He came in just a few months after us. We soon became friends. Over the years we shared many experiences together, exchanged confidences, read, played, discussed, worked, differed, argued. We came from two completely different backgrounds and in many respects had differing ideas and outlooks. We were thrown together in the same confined environment to face common problems and, more important, to gear ourselves for the years that lay ahead. In the process, a close bond developed between us. And this week we had to part, perhaps never to see each other again. We were in the original foursome who started playing bridge surreptitiously at first and with hand made cards. We played a number of other games together. Just a few hours before the boat took him away, we played a couple of rubbers of bridge, we drank tea, ate biscuits, sang a few songs, teased each other and said goodbye. It was a very difficult moment, and we let it pass as quickly as possible.

Censors work in mysterious ways. For reasons known only to themselves, the second paragraph was ordered to be erased.]

29.

"The hardest thing to open is a closed mind."

[29.

We made a key. Not me, but Japhta Masemola, with the help of Mac Maharaj and Laloo Chiba. My job was to keep watch while they were working. Japhta (Jeff) was a PAC chap, while Mac and Laloo were ANC, but in matters such as these political affiliation did not count. Jeff was a genius with his hands. He made carpenters' tools, he made musical instruments, he made our bookcases, he made the key. If I recall correctly, he had a soft piece of soap ready and, when the warder for some reason or other left the key on his desk, Jeff quickly made an imprint; a proper master key that could unlock every lock. And then they started filing. The metal must have been picked up when we were working at the seaside – we also picked up timber for the bookcases, and other flotsam and jetsam. Madiba once picked up a high quality jersey, and he became quite attached to it. I won't be surprised if he came out of prison with it.

Jeff built my bookcase with expertly made false bottoms in the bookcase drawers to hide contraband. They were never detected.

We didn't use the key to open and close our cells. That would have been too risky and dangerous; as would have been any attempt to use it to escape.

At times we used to pick up more than one newspaper from the rubbish dump. Once, I think a bundle of about fifteen – all wet and dirty. There was too much to finish overnight. We opened a cell in the unused centre wing, and hid them there. I took a few at a time to my cell, to glean the information from them and share it. We also stored prohibited books, smuggled in by bribed or blackmailed warders, in that cell.

Eventually, when the security situation worsened, we buried the key in the quarry. I have a rough idea where.]

30.

"People who have wild ideas about how to run the earth ought to start with a small garden."

Reader's Digest, December 1972

[30.

My role in our garden, which we were allowed to start in 1974, was insignificant. On Robben Island the enthusiastic gardeners were Madiba and some of the Indian comrades, who were descendants of peasants, and thus had green fingers.

Laloo Chiba is the most meticulous man I ever met. I once noticed him and his group walking towards the garden, with notebook, ballpoint pen, and other items in hand. I first assumed it was his Economics class, from which he had expelled me. But some questions lingered: why the garden? And why bending down and touching some of the plants? To satisfy my curiosity I sidled up to the group. I'm not exaggerating, it was no Economics class – Chiba was bending down to a chilli plant and attaching a little piece of paper with a rubber band to a couple of chillies. On the label was a note: 'On 20 September (or whatever) this particular chilli measured x millimetres'! And one day he gave me a related task: I had to count, one by one, the number of our tomato seeds. I do not know the reason for it, but I carried out the task as instructed. I think I counted about eight hundred-odd seeds.

In everything he undertakes, Madiba, too, is thorough; when MK started he read as much as possible about guerrilla warfare. When he learnt to play chess he ordered a chess book. So it was with the garden. In his heart he is very much a rural man; his love for plant life never left him. He just had to supplement his early practical experience with literature, and with discussions with some of the warders with a farming background.

The garden became important. There was always a water

shortage on the island; fresh water had to be brought from Cape Town. For this reason warders were not allowed to have gardens; yet we were! Why? Prison logic!

We enjoyed what came out of the garden. Even non-gardeners took an interest. Billy Nair (trade unionist and MK commander) had a cell which overlooked the garden. He jealously guarded the products. One night the usual silence was shattered by Billy loudly shouting, 'Hey, leave that alone!' It was a warder trying to steal one of the precious half-a-dozen or so melons.

When a chameleon suddenly appeared one day, the garden assumed special importance. Parental instincts took over; you'd find young and old swatting flies to feed the poor creature. A whole debate started when, after disappearing for a while, it reappeared with little ones. 'Where is Papa chameleon? Is there a Papa? And how does it reproduce ...?'

When the mother disappeared, leaving the babies behind, everybody turned on her for abandoning them. That was a story about babies in general, whether chameleon or human. Men without women, husbands without wives, fathers without children ...]

31.

"Help us to be always hopeful

Gardeners of the spirit
Who know that without darkness
Nothing comes to birth,
As without light …
Nothing flowers."

Reader's Digest

[31.

The most important thing planted in our garden was memory.

A couple of years before Madiba's sixtieth birthday (in 1978), while walking in the courtyard, Walter and I pondered how best we might celebrate it. We decided that we should tell his story. Madiba agreed.

Madiba symbolised Robben Island, although not of his own volition. He symbolised political imprisonment. Again, not of his own volition. If something went out in his name, it would also inspire people. We didn't have to convince him.

Since the consequences of discovery would be dire – not only for those directly involved, but for the entire prison community – the secret was shared between the leadership and a small, tightknit group only.

Without documents or books all we had to tell the story was memory, so we had to dig deep into the recesses of our minds to free that memory. Fortunately, Walter's knowledge of ANC, and liberation history, was awesome, and his memory prodigious.

Often feigning illness, Madiba stayed away from work, and slept, so that he could keep awake at night to write, and the next morning he would pass on the manuscript to Walter and me for our comments, corrections, and additions. The final version would be passed on to Mac Maharaj and Laloo Chiba who transcribed it in their tiny, meticulous handwriting onto the thin rice paper that I had so fortuitously ordered. These pages (reduced to about fifty–sixty from Madiba's five hundred–six hundred!) were concealed in the covers of the album (containing large maps) that Chiba had constructed for the purpose, and that Mac later openly carried out with him when he was released.

We buried the original in the garden in plastic cocoa containers. But foolishly we didn't destroy it as planned when Mac informed me that the manuscript had reached England safely.

One day, out of the blue, the builders started a wall that was designed to block off part of 'B' section, in order to create a separate 'A' section to accommodate the post-1976 new arrivals.

The wall went through our garden where the plastic containers with Madiba's manuscript were hidden. The fateful earth was turned, and the discovery made, exposing the three conspiratorial worms – Madiba, Walter and me. Our writing was recognisable in the manuscript and for this 'criminal offence' the three of us were punished by having our study privileges cancelled, in the end for four years.]

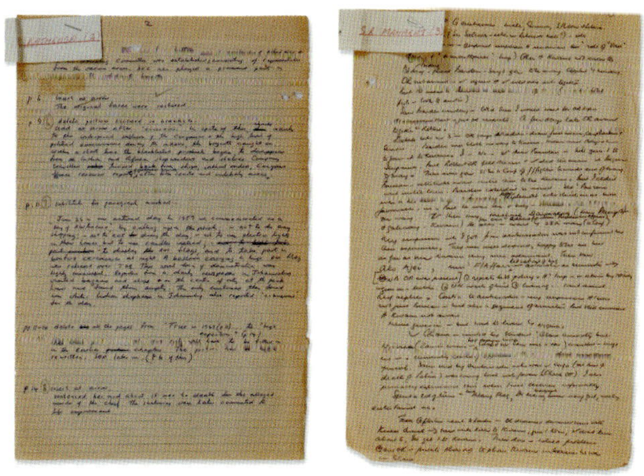

"God preserve us from the exile colonies and the exile conflicts."

Vladimir Ulyanov

[32.

Even in prison you're always conscious you are serving a cause. As Milton said, they also serve who only stand and wait. By being there you are a representative, though I think we did, in the end, achieve more than just being passive. There was the education of many inmates, the smuggled manuscripts and, above all, Madiba's bold political step that initiated the negotiation process, leading eventually to April 1994, and the formation of the first non-racial, non-sexist, democratic government, when I was no longer a pariah in the land of my birth.

I often think of one of the quotations I took down from Lenin. (In my exercise books I used his lesser-known real name – as above – so the authorities might not recognise who the author was.) He rails against life in exile.

Having already endured many years of hardship and basic deprivations I naturally reflected on my own decision not to go into voluntary exile. The information about life in exile that came with MK comrades who joined us on Robben Island only served to confirm that I had been right to remain in South Africa.

I have no regrets that at the time of our release I had spent almost half of my sixty years in prison. Imprisonment and the resistance of the prisoners was after all one of the pillars of our struggle.

I was always conscious of the reality that, as hard as prison life was, it was the comrades outside jail, who had remained in South Africa, who bore the brunt of the struggle. They were at the coalface and were exposed to the dangers of detention, torture and death every minute of their lives. They made us walk tall.

However, any record of our struggle would be incomplete if we did not pay tribute to Oliver Tambo, in particular, and his team of stalwarts – Yusuf Dadoo, J B Marks, Moses Kotane, Thabo Mbeki and Joe Slovo – in exile, for not only holding the ANC together, but more importantly, for successfully mobilising world opinion on the side of our struggle.]

33.

"The moon, ever a companion to me in prison, has grown more

friendly with closer acquaintance, a reminder of the loveliness of this world, of the waxing and waning of life, of light following darkness, of death and resurrection following each other in interminable succession. Ever changing, yet ever the same, I have watched it in its different phases and its many moods in the evening as the shadows lengthen in the still hours of the night, and when the breath and whisper of dawn brings promise of the coming day."

Nehru, *The Discovery of India*

[33.

I cannot claim, honestly, that the moon had this same effect on me as I looked out of my cell window at the night sky.

What did have a startling impact on me, leaving a lasting impression, was the great earthquake (centred on the town of Tulbagh, one hundred and eighty kilometres north-east of Cape Town). This was the night of 29 September 1969 and the quake measured 6.5 on the Richter scale.

The prison bars are round and quite thick, but inside each bar (although we didn't know it till then) there was a rod so that if prisoners tried to cut through, when they reached the rod it would make a noise. But when the earthquake came (we felt the ripple effects strongly on Robben Island) the rods shook and it was a frightening thing. We were locked up. The warder on duty that night did the only sensible thing he could do, because he didn't have the master key. He ran out to get help. All sorts of things went through my mind. I thought there had been a nuclear bomb test. Was the whole island going to be flooded, and we drowned? One of our colleagues actually slept through it!

They took us out to the courtyard. They kept us there for a while, then locked us up again.

That was the first time we saw the stars, maybe the moon, too, not through prison bars.]

"He had always had a curious sense of the insignificance of human effort, even his own. 'It will be as God wills it,' he once said, 'and it's all a matter of time. People and individuals, wisdom and folly, war and peace – they come and go like the waves of the sea while the sea remains.'"

Werner Richter, *Bismarck*

[34·

The International Red Cross used to visit us every year from Geneva, so a day or two before, there'd be no more quarry work; we'd do light work at the seaside pulling seaweeds. Very filthy work, and the seaweed was full of insects. The thing is, though, they did that every year, just before the Red Cross visit. They knew, and we knew, that the day after the Red Cross left, it was back to the quarry. And they knew we were going to tell the Red Cross. The charade continued year after year.

Afterwards they took us to the sea for longer periods – they were not preparing for any visits. We got used to it, and we enjoyed the fresh air and the sea breeze. And that's where we caught limpets and periwinkles, crayfish and perlemoen (abalone), partridges and guinea fowl; once, even a seal that had beached. A few times we managed to get hold of ostrich eggs. We discovered the shell was very hard, and we had to use a stone to crack it open but, if I remember correctly, each egg contained the equivalent of over twenty hen's eggs.

Our lunch was brought in drums; after eating we emptied a drum, filled it with water, boiled it, and dumped our catch of the day into the drum.

It was not even tasty; in fact the perlemoen was like rubber; but it was considered a much sought-after delicacy, and we just had to have a taste. Only once, or at the most, twice, since my release have I eaten it the way it's supposed to be prepared. It was tasty, but I wouldn't pay almost a thousand rand (about US $150) for a perlemoen starter!

We ate the sea and land animals, not so much out of hunger, but more out of mischief, and to break the monotony. It was a wonderful experience. Some of the chaps were even allowed to have a dip in the sea. Relations with the warders had become very cordial by then. Some of them even shared the goodies with us. One day we were caught in the act by Lieutenant Terreblanche. All he said was, 'Take it easy chaps. Don't overdo it.'

Working close to Alpha One (an old building right on the shore-line) we had quite a view, the best of Cape Town you can get, and nowadays favoured by photographers. Today, when I accompany visitors to the island, and when time allows, we make a stop at Alpha One, to savour that view. A glimpse of freedom.]

35.

"The stones that critics hurl

with harsh intent, a man may use to build his monument."

Arthur Guiterman, *Reader's Digest*

[35.

On the way to the boardwalk where the penguins are, there are some huge blocks of concrete, designed for the harbour breakwater. Nowadays I often take my visitors there, and show them the inscription on one block in particular. It says, 'We, the ANC, are sure of victory.' It is an illustration of how confidence and optimism remained uncrushed, right through the bad, and good years. 'We are going to win. One day. When it is going to be we don't know.' That Madiba was going to be president never crossed his mind. Or if it did he never told us. I never ever imagined I was going to be a Member of Parliament, and Parliamentary Counsellor in the president's office. But the optimism that the ANC was going to win, one day, *that* we never lost.

Many years later, while it was still a prison for common-law prisoners, and just before it was declared a National Museum and Heritage Site, the commanding officer, Colonel Elsa Jones, said to me, 'Come, let me show you something,' and it was she who first pointed out the inscription to me. I had not known of it before, though it echoed exactly what I had written to Sylvia in 1964: 'There is no such thing as defeat in our struggle.' I'm sure the man who inscribed it, and the comrades who worked with him, were the only ones who knew of it, but the message was carved into our hearts as surely as it was scored in stone. It will be there for posterity.]

36.

"I don't go along with talk of a generation gap. We are all contemporaries. There's only a difference of memories. That is all."

W H Auden

[36.

Madiba has a sense of humour, but it's of a particular kind. The thing about it is that what he says makes people laugh because he has said it. It's also meant to set people at ease, make them comfortable. If I were to say the same thing people might not laugh! For instance, when I meet Madiba and there are other people there, when he steps into a room and sees me, he says, 'Oh, this crook is here. He sent me to jail.' You laugh because he's said it. I often retort, saying, 'My biggest mistake in life was when I first met you in 1945; I've never been out of trouble since ...' but the effect is never quite the same.

One of my complaints when the five of us were transferred to Pollsmoor Prison in 1982 was that I was going to be locked up with Mission-educated people – Madiba and Raymond Mhlaba in particular, but also Walter and Andrew Mlangeni. They were all older than me. They would tease each other about past situations, and we would enjoy it and laugh. But they didn't swear, and they didn't tell rude jokes. I didn't relish having to spend more years in jail without light-hearted moments when we didn't have to mind our language or the content of our conversations.

Much as I loved and admired these men, I missed the informal meetings of our tea club on Robben Island, in my friend Wilton Mkwayi's cell, with Mike Dingake and another friend, Theo Cholo. This was a daily practice after we stopped going to work. We enjoyed the uninhibited talk, the occasional rude jokes, and swearing. Walter loved his tea, and would just stroll in, and all of us would teasingly exclaim, 'What do you want here, you are not invited!' He would ignore the bantering, smile and simply sit down, and enjoy

36 – Continued

the tea. Of course our interaction in his presence would still be light-hearted, but more carefully tailored. We really loved to have him there. He was always the butt of teasing and banter but forever smiling, never cross.

During my first weeks and months at Pollsmoor, I tried everything possible to get back to Robben Island. I managed to invoke the support of the doctor, as well as the Red Cross. But when nothing helped I quickly adjusted to the inevitable. Was I the only person ever to ask to be sent back to Robben Island?

The Soweto-1976 uprising young men who came to the island were very angry, bitter, full of hatred, and wanting revenge. They had survived after hundreds of their peers were mercilessly killed. They wanted to continue the fight in jail but there were no stones to throw. On one occasion, they managed to get hold of a sharpened spoon, and stabbed an officer, injuring him. Our elders had to persuade them, 'You have lost your liberty; there's nothing you can do about it. You can kill a few warders, but you'll still remain in jail. So you have to adjust yourselves to a positive approach. Make the best of your years. Study and equip yourselves to serve our people.' At last they accepted. And many of these men, including Tokyo Sexwale, are now successful in business, as mayors, provincial ministers, and in other fields.

The Soweto-1976 generation – the pride of our nation.]

"It's really a wonder that I haven't dropped all my ideals, because they seem so absurd and impossible to carry out. Yet I keep them, because in spite of everything I still believe that people are really good at heart. I simply can't build up my hopes on a foundation consisting of confusion, misery and death. I see the world gradually being turned into a wilderness, I hear the ever-approaching thunder, which will destroy us too. I can feel the sufferings of millions and yet, if I look up into the heavens, I think that it will all come right, that this cruelty too will end, and that peace and tranquillity will return again.

In the meantime I must uphold my ideals, for perhaps the time will come when I shall be able to carry them out."

Anne Frank, 15 July 1944, *Diary*

Only two letters follow this entry, 21 July and 1 August 1944. On 4 August 1944, the 'Annexe' (where Anne Frank and her family had been given refuge by a courageous Dutch family) was raided by the Nazi police, and all occupants arrested. They were sent to Auschwitz, and some killed there. Others were transferred to other camps. Anne and her sister Margot contracted typhus in Bergen-Belsen in February 1945, and both died.

[37·

Madiba himself has said somewhere that there comes a time when a leader has to lead. That time arrived for him at Pollsmoor Prison. It required a lot of foresight, and courage. It could have irretrievably hurt his political life.

When we were transferred to Pollsmoor Prison in 1982, we were accommodated together in one large cell, the five of us. Then Madiba was taken away from us.

Instinctively we wanted to protest. But from what I remember (he didn't use these words) he said, 'Cool it chaps, something good may come of this.'

Later we came to know what was going on in his mind. He must have decided that the time had come to talk to the other side. This was consistent with ANC policy. Even when MK was launched there was no expectation of an armed victory. MK, together with the mass struggle in the country, the work of our exiled comrades, and international solidarity, would all combine to force the enemy to come to the negotiation table.

Madiba foresaw that if he was going to consult with us there might be difficulties, he might get opposition. And he's a democrat par excellence, he'll accept a majority decision. So he must have thought, 'Let me take this initiative.' He did. He took the initiative; he started talking. Afterwards, when he reported to us, we mostly supported him, though with some reservations. He found Raymond and Andrew entirely in agreement; Walter and I said there could be no objection in principle. Walter thought the initiative should come from the other side; I thought, in view of the unprecedented mass upsurge of resistance and defiance throughout the country, we would be talking from a position of weakness.

But, in retrospect, he was right and I was wrong. His timing was perfect.]

"Lord, make me an instrument of Thy Peace,
Where there is hatred, let me sow love;
Where there is injury, pardon;
Where there is discord, union;
Where there is doubt, faith;
Where there is despair, hope;
Where there is darkness, light;
Where there is sadness, joy;
O Divine Master, grant that I may not so much seek
To be consoled, as to console;
To be understood, as to understand;
To be loved, as to love;
For it is in giving that we receive;
It is in pardoning that we are pardoned;
And it is in dying that we are born to eternal life."

St Francis of Assisi (+-1181–1226), who renounced wealth and social pre-eminence for a life of utter poverty and fearlessness

[38.

The ideal expressed in the prayer of St Francis – as relevant today as it was eight hundred years ago – is very difficult to attain, but it is something one can strive for. I don't think it's easy to succeed because this requires a very, very special person. A saint. And there are very few such people.

The ANC was confronted with a country where three hundred and fifty years of white rule had caused injury to the majority of people – fertile ground for discord, despair, revenge, hate, and violence.

Nelson Mandela has repeatedly appealed to people not to regard him as a saint. In all his activities as a freedom fighter, and later as chief negotiator, and as president, he was not acting as an individual, but as part of a team. And more importantly, he was implementing the policy of the ANC.

With the powerful, peaceful armoury of non-racialism, democracy, reconciliation, equality, forgiveness, unity; and absence of bitterness, hatred, and revenge, Mandela, in his inimitable style, became the symbol of love, hope and confidence – not only to the people of South Africa, but to the world.

No saint perhaps, but he came so close to putting the humble saint's aspirations into practice, that the saint, if he were to indulge himself just for once, would no doubt be proud of him.]

"While we will not forget

the brutality of apartheid
We will not want Robben Island to be a monument
to our hardship and suffering.

We would want it to be a triumph
Of the human spirit against the forces of evil,
A triumph of wisdom and largeness of spirit against
small minds and pettiness,
A triumph of courage and determination over human
frailty and weakness;
A triumph of the new South Africa over the old."

Ahmed Kathrada, 1993

[39.

Since my release, and as chairperson of the first Robben Island Museum Council, I have been requested to accompany hundreds of groups, as well as individuals, on visits to the island. These are regarded as 'special visits', distinct from the tens of thousands of visitors who come to the island annually, and who are guided by the full-time guides employed by the museum.

I can't recall ever turning down a request to accompany people. I have never felt tired or bored carrying out this task.

At the very outset, I convey to visitors that the moment the ferry departs from Cape Town, and until we return, Robben Island is neutral – neutral in South African, as well as in international, politics. It has been my privilege to convey this message to diverse groups of people and individuals – Clinton and Castro, Hillary Clinton and Barack Obama, Arafat and the World Jewish Congress, Margaret Thatcher and Gerry Adams, the presidents of Uganda, India, Nigeria, Algeria, China; kings and queens of the Nordic countries, as well as President Mbeki and numerous South African cabinet ministers and MPs including Jacob Zuma and his family. From the entertainment world, I have accompanied Jane Fonda, Sidney Poitier, Michael-Jamal Warner, Cecily Tyson, Denzel Washington, Quincy Jones, Oprah Winfrey, Samuel Jackson, Carlos Santana, Janet Jackson, Amitabh Bachchan, Morgan Freeman, Danny Glover, Forest Whitaker, Stevie Wonder and our own Charlize Theron, along with my special friends Alfre Woodard, Pauletta Washington, La Tanya Richardson, and many, many others. The list goes on.

I'm frequently asked by interested persons, what do you think of so and so. My response is uniform. I respect all of them, but one to one, they are all the same.

The person who has undoubtedly made the greatest impact on me was a little girl of about twelve. On one of my visits, she came up to me, and shyly asked, 'Can I have your

39. Continued

autograph, and may I have a photograph with you?' I light-heartedly replied, 'Yes. But only if you pay me.' We both laughed and I took her and her family on the tour. Then someone told me that young Michelle Brits was terminally ill with leukaemia, and that she had two last wishes before she died – to visit Robben Island, and to meet President Mandela.

In Johannesburg, I said to Madiba, 'Look, there's this little girl, can I bring her to you, to the house?' His response was pure, vintage Madiba. He said, 'No, that's too much trouble for her. Let's rather go to her.' So, on the appointed day, he got into his helicopter with gifts for Michelle. She also had gifts for him. The most moving and unforgettable scene was, after the exchange of gifts, Michelle spontaneously put her little arms around his neck, and kissed him. It must have brought tears to the eyes of thousands of television viewers, as it did to mine. I am still unable to talk about Michelle without emotion.

Michelle was an Afrikaner child, from a very right-wing mining town, but she had embraced the message of the new South Africa. By her simple, free gesture of affection she showed, more powerfully than any of the convoluted writings and carefully crafted speeches that are the standard fare of politicians, that our children truly are the future.

Thank you, Michelle. In your last days you enriched more lives than you could ever have imagined, none more so than my own. A beautiful young girl like a steady light in an unsettled sea. To the end of my days I will cherish the memory of our chance encounter on the island.]

"My work is my life.

I cannot think of one without the other. To 'retire' means to me to begin to die. The man who works and is never bored is never old.

Each day I am reborn. For the past eighty years I have started each day in the same manner. It is not a mechanical routine but something essential to my daily life. I go to the piano and I play two preludes and fugues of Bach. It is a sort of benediction on the house. It fills me with awareness of the wonder of life, with a feeling of the incredible marvel of human being. The music is never the same to me. Each day it is something new, fantastic and unbelievable. That is Bach, like nature a miracle."

Prescription for living, by Pablo Casals, world-famous cellist

[40.

Cape Town may be the most beautiful place in the world. I enjoy walking by the sea, which we do every day, Barbara and I. Most mornings, early, we drive to Sea Point and walk for an hour. A simple freedom. But when we start late we walk in the Company Gardens behind Parliament, just across the way from our flat.

It took us twelve years to discover the beauty of that garden but now we walk there often. Barbara is much more aware of this tree and that tree, this plant and that flower than I am. She never fails to show me and tell me their names, and then cross-examines me the next day. What is this tree and that flower? I enjoy that, even if I often fail the exam.]

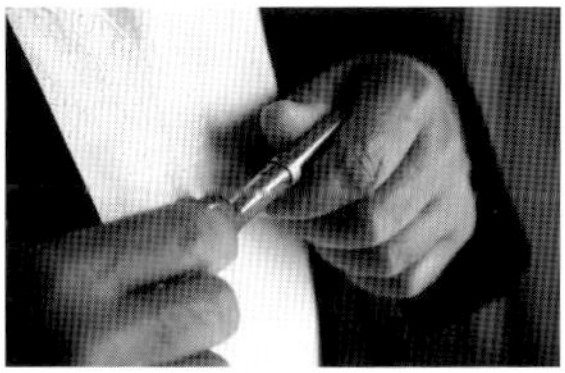

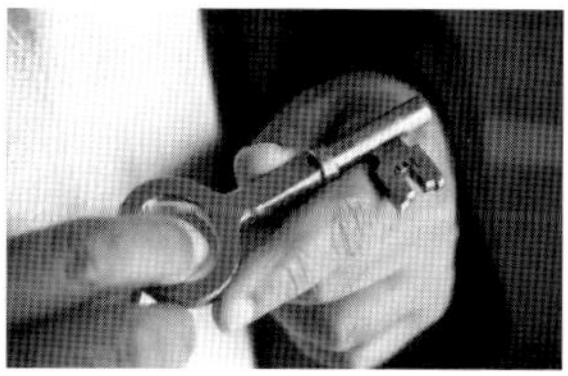

ACKNOWLEDGEMENTS

It's been a pleasure, and a positive learning experience to have had the privilege of working with Tim Couzens during the preparation of this book. We spent much time together, identifying the list of forty quotations, discussing and tape-recording, re-discussing, amending, and finalising, to our mutual satisfaction. What a lesson for me on the virtue of patience, tolerance and diligence!

At our next meeting Tim surprised me with a thickish bundle of papers. It was the transcript of the tape-recording; but not *typed,* as one takes for granted, but neatly and meticulously done in his handwriting! I learn that he doesn't use a computer. Nor does he possess a cell phone.

He becomes number three on my list of friends who have not 'graduated' to these electronic appliances. All three are outstanding individuals, and achievers in their fields – a Nobel laureate in literature, a top human-rights lawyer, and Tim. A poignant reminder that progress and success are still possible with 'old-fashioned' methods.

Tim has a sharp intellect, and masters whatever he undertakes. But he seriously takes into account other views. And if these have merit, he scrupulously avoids imposing his own. He is unassuming, and modest to a fault. Dickens must have had men like Tim in mind when he wrote, 'There is a great man who makes every man feel small. But the real great man is the man who makes every man feel great.'

Tim has a marvellous, dry sense of humour. He is a simple man, and a wonderful, caring human being. Never during our interaction did I feel that I was working with a professor of English literature, as well as an accomplished author of several books. It would have been a serious omission on my part if I failed to acknowledge that without Tim's unwavering interest, guidance and supervision, and overall contribution, I certainly would not have been able to make a meaningful contribution towards *A Simple Freedom.*

Ahmed Kathrada

The publisher would like to thank the following people for their kind and generous assistance: Tim and Diana Couzens; Matthew Willman; Verne Harris, Nelson Mandela Centre of Memory and Dialogue, Nelson Mandela Foundation; Caroline Bowron; and Anant Singh and Helena Spring, Videovision Entertainment.

The introduction by Nelson Mandela in this book is gleaned largely from his foreword in *Memoirs* (by Ahmed Kathrada) with some additions from his foreword in *Letters from Robben Island – A Selection of Ahmed Kathrada's Prison Correspondence, 1964–1989.*

A further selection of quotations might be found in *A Free Mind – Ahmed Kathrada's Notebook from Robben Island,* edited by Sahm Venter and published by Jacana Media. For a detailed history of Kathy's life see his autobiography, *Memoirs,* published by Zebra Press. For further letters see *Letters from Robben Island – A Selection of Ahmed Kathrada's Prison Correspondence, 1964–1989,* also published by Zebra Press.

The quotations that Kathy took down in his notebooks were transcribed under the constrained circumstances of prison. Original sources or authors' names have been in some cases difficult to verify. The quotation on p. 60 appears to be from G K Chesterton's book *Charles Dickens,* rather than being a quote by Dickens himself as recorded in the notebooks. The quotation on p. 64 seems to originate from Thomas Moore's ballad 'Oh, The Sight Entrancing'. The quotation on p. 119 found in *Reader's Digest* originates from May Sarton's poem 'Invocation to Kali'.

First North American edition published by The University Press of Kentucky

Scholarly publisher for the Commonwealth, serving Bellarmine University, Berea College, Centre College of Kentucky, Eastern Kentucky University, The Filson Historical Society, Georgetown College, Kentucky Historical Society, Kentucky State University, Morehead State University, Murray State University, Northern Kentucky University, Transylvania University, University of Kentucky, University of Louisville, and Western Kentucky University.

Editorial and Sales Offices: The University Press of Kentucky
663 South Limestone Street, Lexington, Kentucky 40508-4008
www.kentuckypress.com

ISBN 978-0-8131-6726-8 (hardcover : alk. paper)

This book is printed on acid-free paper meeting the requirements of the American National Standard for Permanence in Paper for Printed Library Materials.

Printed and bound in South Korea by PACOM KOREA Inc.

Member of the Association of American University Presses